FIONA KERLOGUE is Deputy Keeper of Anthropology and Curator
of Asian Collections at the Horniman Museum, London. She holds a PhD
in Southeast Asian Studies (Anthropology) from the University of Hull
and as well as contributing to *Asian Studies Review* her publications
include *Batik: Design, Style & History* (2004).

Thames & Hudson world of art

This famous series provides the widest available
range of illustrated books on art in all its aspects.

If you would like to receive a complete list
of titles in print please write to:

THAMES & HUDSON
181A High Holborn
London WC1V 7QX

In the United States please write to:

THAMES & HUDSON INC.
500 Fifth Avenue
New York, New York 10110

Printed in Singapore

Fiona Kerlogue

Arts of Southeast Asia

183 Illustrations, 102 in color

 Thames & Hudson world of art

1 (*frontispiece*) Statue of the goddess Prajnaparamita from Candi Singasari, East Java, dated to c. 1300, a time when Hinduism and Buddhism both received royal patronage in Central Java. The statue is believed to be a portrait of Putri Dedes, wife of the first king of Singasari.

First published in 2004 in paperback in the United States of America by Thames & Hudson Inc., 500 Fifth Avenue, New York, New York 10110

thamesandhudsonusa.com

Library of Congress Catalog Card Number 2004102646
ISBN 0-500-20381-4

Designed by Sally Jeffery
Printed and bound in Singapore by C.S. Graphics

Contents

Introduction

In the last forty years or so there have been great changes in our understanding of the art of Southeast Asia. Perspectives have altered in the light of fresh research and there has been an increasing appreciation of work that falls outside the confines of the old Hindu-classical evaluation of Southeast Asian art. The work of writers from within the region has also broadened the scope of critical debate. New insights into the artistic worlds of early inhabitants of the region have been made possible through recent archaeological excavations and technical developments in the analysis of finds. The range and extent of the bold patterns on the prehistoric pottery found at Ban Chiang in Thailand [3], for example, was unimaginable until the site was excavated in the 1970s. The Neolithic site of Peinan in Taiwan, discovered at the end of the nineteenth century, was not fully investigated until 1980. With the restoration of peace and the opening up of countries like Cambodia, Laos and Vietnam in the late twentieth century, western scholars have also been able to share new research relating to ancient monuments and works held in

2 Aspects of the material culture of the Naga people of Assam have clear links with other groups in Southeast Asia. The symbolic opposition of textiles and headhunting occurred also among the Iban of Borneo, and the feathers of the hornbill have a similar importance in headdresses, for example. Cloth of merit normally worn as a mantle; cotton and cowrie shells. 1505 × 876 mm.

3 The Prehistoric site at Ban Chiang in northeast Thailand, discovered in 1966, is thought to have been occupied for some 5,000 years. The most well known finds are the baked-clay pots painted with elegant swirling designs, dating from the period 300 BC to AD 200.

museums within the region. The rapprochement with China has also led to opportunities to study more closely the relationship between the art of that great country and that of Southeast Asia. Political and social changes in the region have also given rise to a new generation of artists who have brought fresh vigour and energy into the field, both drawing on and challenging existing traditions. At the same time, the thrust of western analysis of art has changed, with a stronger emphasis on the role of context and culture – political and social – in framing the articulation of ideas. It is these developments which have provided the impetus for this book.

The term 'Southeast Asia' is now generally used to refer to the countries belonging to the organization ASEAN, the Association of Southeast Asian Nations. Whether it is appropriate to consider this group as a whole in terms of its art and culture is another question. Geography and language divide the region into

4 View of the main tower of Prasat Phnom Rung, a 12th-century Shivaite Khmer sanctuary, seen from the west. A replica of the Shiva lingam can be seen in its original position at the centre of the principal prang.

two main parts: the maritime region, which includes the insular and peninsular parts of Malaysia, Brunei, Singapore, the Indonesian archipelago and the Philippines, and the mainland, which includes Burma, Laos, Thailand, Cambodia and Vietnam. Political boundaries do not correspond precisely with cultural patterns however, which derive in part from ancient patterns of migration. In the prehistoric period, speakers of Austronesian languages from Southwest China moved southwards through the islands, bringing with them cosmological beliefs, language, kinship systems, material culture and artistic forms that left a lasting legacy. Later, speakers of the Tai group of languages, again from the north, travelled and settled along the valleys of the mainland. Cultural links extend to some of the people of the Assam hills in India to the northwest [2], to indigenous people of the Andaman islands and to some of the peoples of the islands of Oceania. Neither should Taiwan's part in the spread of Austronesian culture during the Prehistoric period be overlooked.

The influence of world religions has forged links between some cultures within the region and defines differences between others. Hinduism and Buddhism [4], two faiths so closely connected that they are in many ways inseparable, were brought to both mainland and insular Southeast Asia at around the same time, coexisting in many early kingdoms for a period. But the degree to which they took root varied considerably. In the mainland, Buddhism became established in many centres, gathering adherents until it became the dominant religion from Burma in the west to Vietnam in the east. The majority of the people of the islands, on the other hand, subsequently adopted either Islam or, in lesser numbers, Christianity [5]. Indigenous beliefs retain their strong hold in many societies, often inextricably intertwined with elements of the newer religions. The island of Bali has developed its own distinctive form of Hinduism.

While broad similarities of language and religion define the respective cultures of the mainland and the islands, there is considerable diversity in underlying patterns of culture, which affect artistic expression both materially and in symbolic ways. There are hundreds of ethnic groups, identifiable by their different languages, costumes, beliefs or practices. Patterns of kinship, economic activity, social governance, custom and ritual vary widely across the region, and these differences are often expressed artistically in material form as well as in performance.

Nonetheless, there are enough features common to peoples and cultures across the region to justify considering it as a whole.

5 An image of Christ is set against a traditional Kenyah design so that the two merge in an expression of life and resurrection. Such seamless incorporation of imagery from the outside world into existing artistic discourse is typical of the syncretism of Southeast Asian art. Church of Long San, upper Baram river, Sarawak.

Both the islands and the mainland lie squarely on two major trade routes, maritime and overland, between East and West. Since at least the start of the first millennium AD, ships carrying cargoes between China and India have stopped at ports along the coast of Southeast Asia to barter and exchange, providing a rich source of revenue to local rulers. An abundance of natural products – timber, resins and animal products from the forests of the hinterland, precious stones and metal ores from the mountains and river beds, and spices from the eastern islands – have also supplied overseas demand and brought wealth to the region. Rich rulers close to the mouths of the rivers (early ports) controlled the overseas trade, exchanging luxury imports for the products supplied from upstream. This pattern of interaction with foreigners and the resulting relationships between downstream rulers and upstream inhabitants was repeated throughout Southeast Asia, resulting in a plethora of shared artistic forms influenced by the trade in overseas goods.

Differences of geography have created contrasting patterns of agriculture and thus social systems across the region. In the mountainous uplands the land lent itself to swidden cultivation, in which fields were cut from the forest, planted for a few seasons and then left fallow to recover. The land needed to provide for each family stretched a considerable distance, so the size of community that could govern itself as a stable unit was relatively small. These upland regions thus evolved patterns of chieftaincies, usually dominated by lineage heads. In contrast, the lowland plains and valleys were fed by rivers carrying rich and fertile waters, allowing for wet rice cultivation, which yielded much heavier crops. Denser populations grew up, and with them the opportunity for leaders to accumulate surplus rice and so power: individuals, families or villages could specialize in craft production or other activities, their products exchanged for food grown by others. Armies could be fed and workers enlisted to build irrigation systems, towns and later, cities. It was from these lowland settlements that highly stratified societies began to develop, and these eventually grew into city states with courts. Much of the early artistic production that has survived from Indonesia as well as Cambodia, Vietnam, Burma and Thailand originated from these courts.

Studies of Southeast Asian art once focused almost entirely on the monumental architecture and sculpture of these ancient kingdoms [6]. Underpinning this focus was the assumption, sometimes unexplored, that artistic sensibilities are confined to a

6 Stone image of the Buddha in situ at Wat Rathchanabura, Ayutthaya. Images such as these retain their sacredness, even though the building is in ruins.

particular sector of society. The result was a concentration on rare treasures made for the ruling classes or the courts to the exclusion of an enormous range of material produced by and for other sectors of society. Yet Southeast Asian rulers often drew the craftsmen who worked for them from outlying rural areas, and the dichotomy between fine and folk art that is recognized in the western world is not always so clear nor so significant. Most

7 The main features of images of the Buddha have remained constant over many centuries, based on descriptions from the scriptures. This bronze figure from northern Thailand is in the earth-touching mudra, representing the moment of victory over Mara, the forces of delusion, and the attainment of enlightenment. Height 760 mm.

critics now embrace in their definition of art a much wider field of media, including those from both court and countryside, and a broader time span, from the Bronze Age to the present day.

Early studies by western scholars of the Hindu-Buddhist art and architecture of Southeast Asia placed it very much in relation to Indian prototypes, an emphasis that is now seen to have been too heavy. From the early centuries of the first millennium, ideas from India were introduced and incorporated into Southeast Asian cultures, but the term 'Indianization', once widely used to describe this process, is now regarded as far too sweeping. The integration of Indian concepts was neither so deep nor so pervasive as was once thought, and there is evidence of a long and subtle interplay in which the flow was not entirely in one direction. Nevertheless, the elements of expression that did find their way from India into the repertoire of Southeast Asian culture have been long-lasting and pervasive and must be recognized in any account of the arts of the region. In contrast, although there have been points where the histories of Europe and Southeast Asia have intersected, European influence has until recently been negligible.

Southeast Asian artists were always selective in adopting and adapting the ideas, techniques and materials that reached them over the centuries, whether from India or China, from within the region or from further afield. These artists already had strong local traditions, which even now continue to form the base from which more recent modes of expression have developed. However, these traditions were never static. Iconography, processes of manufacture, ritual practices and their associated material culture were in an almost continual state of flux and innovation.

Questions of chronology, of tracing the development of style, also present particular problems in the examination of Southeast Asian art. Architectural styles are eclectic, and where documentary evidence is scarce it is sometimes hard to date buildings or sculptures with accuracy. The construction of monuments founded many centuries ago may have taken place over a long period of time. Many have been added to or partially demolished in the intervening centuries, with results that are often at variance with the concepts underlying the original building. Their functions have often changed over time, and while many ancient places of worship continue to serve a religious community, this may be one practising a different religion. Some still serve as places of pilgrimage, but not all pilgrimages today will have the same goals.

Sculptural forms, especially on the mainland, tended to follow established norms, often deliberately reproducing long-established models [7]. The imagery of ancient art is often reformulated in contemporary work so that past ages have a continuing presence. In such a context, the assignation of a date to a particular work on the basis of style as if there had been a clear line of development, a kind of artistic evolution that echoes the evolution of species, is clearly not relevant and certainly not useful. In many Southeast Asian contexts, such notions of linear progression in art or attempts to identify a work in terms of its place of origin, its human creator or the date it was made would be regarded as an irrelevant and fruitless undertaking.

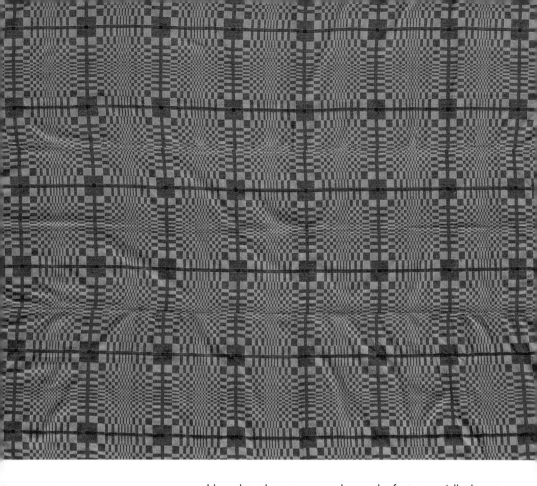

8 Detail of a binakol blanket from the Abra region of the Philippines. 2185 × 1670 mm.

Ideas about how to approach a work of art, especially the art of non-western cultures, have changed enormously over the last few decades. When a western person looks at the art of Southeast Asia, there are some aspects that might be appreciated by a local observer in much the same way. The presence of balance, harmony, contrast and symmetry, for example, can be recognized by any observer, since humans seem to share psychological responses to such phenomena. Similarly, the perception and aesthetic appreciation of repetition, of combinations of colour, of subtleties of line and curve, and of contrasts of light and shade seem to be less a matter of culture than of basic human cognition. The meanings assigned to such artistic phenomena may vary, however. The striking *binakol* blankets of the Tinguian of Northern Luzon [8], for example, which so dazzle the eyes that a spectator may go into trance and enter the spirit world, are very different in context from Op Art designs produced by twentieth-century western artists, despite a sometimes strong superficial resemblance.

For some aspects of artistic meaning there are marked correspondences across cultures. The significance of the planets, especially the sun and moon and their associations with day and night, life and death, man and woman, carry similar resonances in most parts of the world. The association of white with purity, red with blood and black with death occurs frequently but not universally. In Southeast Asia the occurrence of all three of these colours together is associated in some places with the Hindu trinity of Shiva, Vishnu and Brahma, in others with the basic substances from which human life is formed; in many places the three together represent totality [9].

The western observer thus needs to recognize that Europeans and Southeast Asians have very different understandings about the world and the place of art within it, which derive from different environments and different histories. Both traditions recognize the ability of aesthetics to create power, value and meaning above the everyday. In the west, this category of 'art' has come to relate to material objects that may be appreciated in isolation from social context and which serve no utilitarian function. In Southeast Asia the category is both broader and more elusive. Aesthetic criteria and spiritual power there might equally be associated with ephemeral media such as the multicoloured rice-paste constructions [10] offered at temple festivals in Bali or the tattoos on the legs and arms of a Bornean man or woman [11]. Where an

9 Images of roosters carved on a house in Tana Toraja in Sulawesi. The combination of black, red and white carries symbolic significance throughout the region.

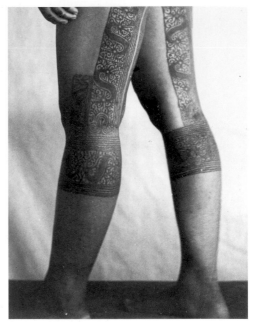

10 The women who make this type of household offering have considerable freedom of artistic interpretation within the basic conventions. Once the gods and demons have extracted the essence, the material remains of the offering are eaten by the family. Karangasem, Bali.

11 Tattoos on the legs of a Kenyah woman. Hendrik Tillema took this photograph on his journey to the Apo Kayan in Borneo, 1931–33. He wrote that after death the soul is examined by a watchman, before crossing the bridge into the next world, where it is reunited with the souls of ancestors. For this, the tattoos must be complete, so that they radiate light to show the way.

art object is substantial, it may be regarded primarily as a shell to be entered by a spirit, and the surfaces of artefacts conceived in part as a kind of screen behind and beyond which a deeper reality operates.

There is also a disparity in ideas about what materials and media constitute the stuff of artistic heritage. Where western notions of art have been founded on ideas from the Greco-Roman Classical period and developed during the Renaissance, Southeast Asian understandings derive more from Indian treatises and from indigenous concepts relating to supernatural power. In the absence of a body of painting ascribed to individual artists, western studies of Southeast Asian art have tended to focus on architecture and sculpture from the ancient period, which could be seen to correspond with ancient Indian artworks. Other media of artistic expression that did not fit into this kind of classification were ignored or categorized as craft rather than art. The tendency for artists not to sign their work, and for artefacts to be produced collaboratively by a number of contributors, also led to such work being largely excluded from western accounts. Neither did the idea of art as the product of creative genius find much correspondence with traditional Southeast Asian attitudes to the artist's role, although works of art were at times undertaken by individuals who had reached a heightened state of some kind, whether in terms of religious purity or connection with other worlds through trance [15]. In Bali the view was widely held that the producer of fine work was acting as a medium for a higher power (*taksu*) which was the true originator of that work. This idea is reiterated in similar forms throughout the region, and does have some resonance with past attitudes in Europe, where artists were sometimes believed to be acting under divine inspiration; indeed, the shift from a belief in divine inspiration to the recognition of creative genius may be an expression of the growing secularization of western society.

The idea that art is something separate from the everyday world is in Southeast Asia a relatively recent introduction. In the majority of cultures in the region art has been seen for the most part as an integral part of daily life, in which the products of skilled craftsmanship have been appreciated in stylistic and aesthetic terms but their role has been primarily functional. Artefacts have never been made simply to be admired for themselves. Although the application of elaborate decoration to an object may indicate that its primary function is ceremonial, this is not always the case [12].

One distinctive aspect of approaches to art in Southeast Asia lies in attitudes to visibility itself. Where the western tradition privileges the visual sense over others and criticism of a work has focused on its visible attributes, in Southeast Asia it is often the invisible, what is being alluded to, that is the most important element. The unseen non-material world, in Bali referred to as

12 Ifugao wood carvers decorate a range of everyday objects, especially those associated with feasting, such as bowls and spoons. Philippines. Heights 163–193 mm

niskala, is inhabited by all kinds of gods and demons, spirits and monsters of earth and sky, and is both real and ever-present. These beings may be addressed through material objects, the importance of which is not in what they look like but how well they can communicate with the world beyond. Thus the primary intention behind the bronze gongs of Dong Son [14], usually referred to as drums, was probably not for them to be looked at but to be struck, so that the reverberation of the sound would summon the spirits of the ancestors. The drums became items of prestige and developed new meanings in different contexts; among the Lamet of Laos, for example, they were a sign of the wealth and thus status that gave their owners access to membership of the ruling group in the community. The sound which they evoked, however, like the aromatic smells of incense and the fragrance of flowers, could penetrate the unseen world inhabited by spirits who could influence the lives of the living. The invisibility of these spirits is regarded as key to their potency, and insubstantiality is to some extent key to the power of art.

The distinction between art and the everyday is probably less clearly demarcated in Southeast Asia than it is in the west. Indeed the words used in Indonesia, Thailand and other parts of the region that are normally translated as 'art' have different

13 Carved wooden figure, Southeast Maluku, Indonesia. In the past, squatting figures were placed at the top of altars, some carrying bowls for offerings to ancestors; some might represent founders or guardians of the village. Height 585 mm.

14 Bronze drums continue to have significance in many parts of Southeast Asia, whether at royal temples in Cambodia or in village contexts. Luang island, eastern Indonesia.

15 Trance dancer, Wonosobo, East Java. The dancer is possessed by a spirit that has entered his body; the mask allows him to take on its persona.

16 Parompa sadum from Sumatra, c. 1991. 2262 × 720 mm.

connotations and tend to stretch much further than they do in the west. Such words generally refer as much to craftsmanship and decorative art, and performances such as music and dance, as they do to the so-called 'fine arts'; art can be ephemeral, evanescent, and it can be found at all levels of society. However, where societies became stratified the upper echelons often set down standards by which artistic expression was judged. In Java, it was the *priyayi*, the gentry, who were most concerned with matters of artistic discrimination, and many of the concepts that traditionally shaped their worldview became criteria of aesthetic judgment in wider society. The terms *alus* and *kasar* refer to a range of metaphysical and social qualities, whether they relate to etiquette, language, a piece of batik cloth or a dancer's performance. *Alus* describes something refined, smooth, finely worked, subtle or allusive, while *kasar* is its opposite: something rough, crude or vulgar. These classifications are still used in judgments about art, with members of the priyayi class or its modern equivalent generally deferred to as arbiters of taste. In the stratified societies of mainland Southeast Asia too, as art becomes a commodity it is regarded increasingly as the preserve of the aristocracy, the landed gentry or the newly rich. In lowland Buddhist societies on the mainland the connection between art and the ruling class was more prominent, through the sponsorship of *wat* or temple building, the embellishment of the wat with murals [17], and the donation of Buddha images and other religious artefacts, but other members of society undertook work with a similar purpose

17 Scenes of hell from the walls of Wat Phra Singh, Chiang Mai, northern Thailand. Such murals convey moral messages to devotees, as well as conferring merit on the sponsor.

(albeit on a smaller scale). Throughout the region there is vigorous production of work by and for all classes and in a range of media, judged and valued according to artistic criteria.

Critics from outside the region seeking elucidation of iconographic references have in the past been beset with problems of interpretation. The propensity in Southeast Asia for importing motifs and transforming their meanings has caused untold confusion to those expecting to find that Indian or Chinese readings have been transplanted intact. Further, as elsewhere in the world, images and iconography are interpreted by different groups in different ways, and interpretations often vary also from one individual to another within a group. Thus human figures may represent ancestors or slaves [13], or they may be vehicles into which a sickness spirit is invited to enter, before it is dispatched to the waters of a river or to flames in order to destroy the disease [18]. The depiction of a serpent may refer to a Hindu deity or a figure in Buddhist legend, or it may refer more loosely to the watery domain or ancestral beings. The idea that meanings can be 'read' from motifs as if in a codified language is not always appropriate to Southeast Asian art, in which efficacy may be more important than meaning. This is not to say that such codification does not exist: in some cases an object contains messages expressed in a precise syntax which can be elucidated by an expert. In North Sumatran weavings such as the *abit godang* or 'great cloth', or the *parompa sadum* [16], a cloth used by the Angkola Batak people to hold a baby, moral messages and references to events in the life of the owner are clearly embedded in the motifs and their arrangement. In other cases the meaning lies not in the motifs but in how the item is used, where it is placed or to whom it is given. Meanings may be multilayered and complex; they may even be deliberately elusive. In some cases, the power of the object lies precisely in its inscrutability.

One core idea that is widespread throughout Southeast Asia is the belief that art objects may be invested with power. Many figures are crafted with the intention that invisible entities may enter them so that they can then be addressed in some way [19]. The entity may be the spirit of an illness, in which case the figure can be destroyed (and with it the disease). Or the entity may be a deity, invited to enter the figure so that offerings and prayers may be made to it. Other artefacts may be permanently imbued with some kind of intrinsic power, and protective talismans are common throughout mainland Southeast Asia and in the archipelago.

18 A *Bes Musang* (civet cat) wood carving by Yaman. This nocturnal forest spirit causes various kinds of pain. During the 1960s, the Jahut people were encouraged to produce replicas of their sickness figures. Pahang, Malaysia. Height 210 mm.

Notions concerning the nature of art vary not just between western audiences and those of Southeast Asia, but also within the region itself. But what is clear is that the interpretation of these products of Southeast Asian makers requires an approach that recognizes local understandings and underlying beliefs. That most of the art of Southeast Asia is closely linked to religious and spiritual life makes it especially difficult for someone unfamiliar with those cultures to fully comprehend it. The peoples of this region have a complex history of religious syncretism with myriad variations across the region. Most of the population of the mainland now adheres to Buddhism, while in the archipelago the majority follows Islam, but there are a great many exceptions. At the same time these major religions have taken different forms over the centuries, subsuming pre-existing beliefs and variously adapting to influences from the world beyond, so that the result is a complex melding of ideas which interlock and overlap in an endless variety of permutations. For this reason, an analysis that takes as its starting point the earliest examples of artwork to survive, and then traces the religious themes that run as threads through the region's histories and cultures, is as likely as any to successfully guide the reader to an appreciation of the region's art.

19 A Taoist priest paints the eyes of an image of the opium god to signify that its spirit has entered the effigy. Festival of the Hungry Ghosts, Penang, Malaysia, 2000.

Chapter 1   Origins

The earliest human inhabitants of Southeast Asia lived largely by foraging. Some exploited the coastal resources along the shores of the region while others lived in caves close to the streams and forests of the interior. These people developed a close relationship with the natural world on which they relied for their existence. Their earliest manipulation of materials was confined to fashioning tools such as axes and arrowheads, traps and nets. These early cultures depended for the most part on stone tools, which archaeologists have labelled Hoabhinian after a type site at Hoa Bình in Vietnam. Many of these tools demonstrate considerable skill in their manufacture but there is little evidence of an artistic sensibility at work until the last two millennia BC.

The period of Neolithic technology, which developed between 4000 and 1000 BC in coastal and lowland parts of mainland Southeast Asia, left evidence of growing expertise in a variety of media. Polished stone adzes [21] display a real command of the technology and while their forms would have been determined largely by function, the elegant flow of the shapes suggests an appreciation on the part of the makers of the quality of the surface texture. Stone bracelets from this period may have been intended as merely symbolic, perhaps of protection or status, but their forms imply the beginnings of a concern with adornment that is clearly aesthetic. Most of the evidence we have comes from excavations in Thailand. At Ban Kao, a site that dates from the middle of the second millennium BC, the distinctive T-section of the bracelets is not determined by function, and the range of materials used to produce such bracelets, in slate, marble and shell, shows consideration for colour, texture and pure form.

Shell was used during the Neolithic period to make other decorative artefacts such as ear ornaments [23] and beads. At Khok Phanom Di, in Thailand, the remains were found of one woman who had been buried with more than 100,000 shell beads,

20 Ochre paintings on the rock face at Pha Thaem overlooking the Mekong river in northeastern Thailand.

21 Neolithic adzes made from semi-precious stones were probably used as ritual tokens. Adze in polished calcedony, found in Sukabumi, West Java. 130 × 61 × 14 mm.

25

22 Burnished pot from Khok Phanom Di, Thailand.

23 An ear ornament carefully crafted from shell. Ban Mai Chai Mongkohn, Nakhon Sawan, Thailand. Diameter 80 mm.

probably attached to clothing, which would have shimmered in the sun. The love of reflected light is a continuing theme in Southeast Asian art, and is also evident in some of the pottery [22] found at the same site, which had been burnished by rubbing the surface with a smooth tool such as a pebble before firing. The result is a surface sheen that can have had no practical function; it is clearly an aesthetic elaboration.

The great range of pottery found at sites all over the mainland, but especially in Thailand, presents the most interesting evidence of artistic endeavour from the Neolithic period is . At Khok Phanom Di, occupied from around 2000 BC to 1600 BC, pots were shaped by beating the clay with a paddle, a technique still widely used in the region today. Decorative effects were produced in a variety of ways: some surfaces were impressed with the texture of cord, probably wrapped around the paddle, some were incised and some burnished. The shapes into which the clay was formed were partly dictated by the use for which the pots were intended, but the elegance of line and curve and the great variety suggest that aesthetic considerations also came into play. The complexity of the decorative designs is also remarkable, and there is some consistency of style within particular sites which suggests that preferential choices were made and that these were generally agreed. That the skill of the potter was highly valued is suggested by the wealth of pottery buried as grave goods. Furthermore, some graves of individuals of high status – judging by the care with which they were buried and the quantity of goods buried with them – included their tools of trade; many of these individuals seem to have been potters.

26

Some sites had particular styles of their own. At Ban Kao a number of distinctive pots with high pedestals and tripod supports were found, in particular a carinated cooking pot supported on cord-marked tripod legs. At Ban Tha Kae the motifs incised on the surface of the pots were accentuated by cord marking [24], either within the motifs or in the areas surrounding them. In general, the background and foreground balance one another in both area and shape, another characteristic of Southeast Asian art that is still evident today. Other sites yielded different techniques: at Nok Nok Tha some of the graves contained painted pottery, while at Non Mak La a striking pot shaped into the form of a cow was found [25].

Figurines in the shape of animals and humans have been found in a number of sites on the mainland, and these probably reflect the importance of the animals so depicted. They include pigs, deer and elephants, but most prevalent are buffalo and other bovine forms.

In maritime Southeast Asia the earliest evidence of art is found in Neolithic remains associated with cultural expansion from Southern China through Taiwan and into the archipelago some four thousand years ago. The early Yuanshan culture of eastern Taiwan left a range of decorated pottery vessels, some slipped in red or brown, others decorated with incised patterns or dentate motifs impressed with stamps. At Peinan, thousands of objects were found in graves made from stone slabs. Finds included plain orange pottery, pig and dog figurines as well as items made from a local material called Taiwan jade (tremolitic nephrite). From this material there were necklaces made of tubular pieces, earrings [26],

24 Sketches of incised decorative motifs on Neolithic vessels from Ban Tha Kae.

25 A pot found at a Neolithic site at Non Mak La, Thailand, in 1994. The pot is decorated with incised lines.

hair ornaments and bracelets. Some of these ornaments were formed into the shapes of animals, while others were geometric. Perhaps the most significant were the split earrings of a type known as *ling-ling-o* [27]. These nephrite ornaments have four outward projections from the circumference. Earrings of this type have been found also in the Guangdong region of southern China, the Philippines, Sarawak, southern Thailand and southern Vietnam. This distribution coincides with the direction of migration of Austronesian-speakers, some of whom are believed to have sailed from Taiwan to the Philippines and beyond. Aspects of their culture spread west to Borneo and later to Java, Sumatra and to the coast of the Malay Peninsula, and southwards and to the east into Sulawesi and the eastern islands of Indonesia.

Further south than Luzon, however, the pottery was plain or red-slipped until about 1500 BC, when new styles appeared in the eastern islands of Southeast Asia. Curved and geometrical incisions arranged in discrete zones and stamped designs appeared alongside and partly replaced the existing forms. Some of these developments were probably related to links between Timor, Sulawesi, Sabah and the Philippines and cultures in the Pacific region; similar styles are also found in the Lapita material of Melanesia and Polynesia, the Lapita peoples probably having colonized those islands from the west.

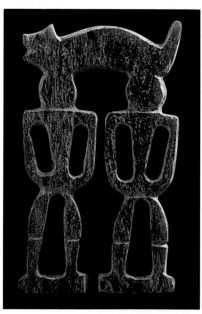 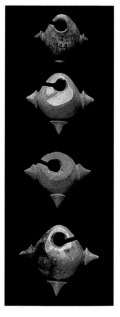

26 Carved jade earring from a Neolithic grave in Peinan, Taiwan, in the form of two standing human figures linked by the figure of an animal.

27 Ling-ling-o earrings from the Sa Huynh culture, central Vietnam.

The most significant technological development in the Prehistoric period was the introduction of methods of bronze production, which in Thailand seems to have begun soon after 1500 BC. Socketed bronze axes have been found dating from this period, probably used for clearing the forest and for cutting and shaping timber for house-building. There were also spearheads and arrowheads, used either as weapons against human enemies or for hunting game. These tools and weapons were mainly cast using bivalve moulds made of sandstone or clay, their form determined primarily by function. Aesthetic considerations may have been more relevant in the design of bronze ornaments such as the bracelets that form the bulk of early finds. Many of these were cast using the lost wax method, and it is clear that early bronze workers quickly became proficient in a range of techniques. Bracelets and anklets were probably symbolic of status or rank, as were ornaments made from iron, which came into use in the mainland in the late Bronze Age, from around 500 BC onwards. Iron objects were usually made by smiths who heated the ore and beat it into shape.

At Ban Na Di, also in Thailand, remains have been found of bronze-working equipment, including a furnace and ceramic

28 Some Bronze Age material echoed the shapes and decorative elements of earlier times. This container with a trumpet-shaped mouth is covered with a red slip. Ban Lum Khao, Thailand.

crucibles, dated to at least 1000 years BC. However, bronze artefacts were not necessarily the most significant or valuable to these cultures. The burial of a child under a crocodile skin and a bone pendant made from a crocodile skull suggests that animals played an important part in symbolic expression, perhaps in totemic terms. Cattle also seem to have had great significance, their bones, probably from sacrifice, buried in many graves. Of the local and exotic ceramics found at this site, most striking were the numerous clay figurines [29] found in the graves, many of cattle, but also of pigs, dogs, elephants and human beings. These figures are modelled with great skill and delicacy, their forms depicted with a sensitivity to the shapes of the living creatures. This importance was sustained over subsequent millennia, with the water buffalo becoming a symbol of status especially in areas of wet rice cultivation, and the central element in status feasts. Strikingly similar figurines dating from the nineteenth century have been found in the Naga hills on the borders of Burma and India.

At Ban Na Di there is also evidence that silk was available. Silk fabric was later to become a medium of artistic expression in Thailand, though whether it was being manufactured locally is uncertain. The ores used for bronze were certainly obtained from elsewhere. There is further evidence of trade or exchange in the

29 Clay figurines of cattle discovered in the Bronze Age cemetery at Ban Na Di, Thailand.

range of exotic materials from which ornaments were fashioned during the Bronze Age. Bracelets [30] were made during this period from carnelian, talc, serpentine and jade, all from far afield but in very similar designs, which suggests that at least some were made locally. The value placed on the material from which items were made, especially when they were brought in from sources of power in distant lands, continued to be an integral part of the complex matrix in which artefacts were framed and understood in Southeast Asia in the ensuing centuries [28].

The most well known and visually striking artefacts from the late Bronze Age in Thailand are the painted funerary vessels from Ban Chiang [3, 31]. Earlier potters at this settlement had produced

30 Bangles made of exotic materials such as slate and marble were found in Bronze Age graves at Ban Na Di.

ceramics with increasingly sophisticated decoration, including white or rust-coloured painted carinated vases with incised patterns on the shoulders. Now the decoration was achieved with rust-coloured patterns painted on a buff base in a variety of designs that responded to the plastic volume of the artefact. Whorls and spirals following the contours of the gently rounded vessels filled the surfaces in a wide range of linear variations, characterized by evenly spaced brushwork forming stripes curving firmly across the clay. The feet and necks of the vessels frequently signalled a change in the direction of the brushwork, the design planned to fit precisely the shape of the available surface area. The graphic idiom of the painters' style is remarkably coherent, with a strong sense of control and a sure deliberation in the placement of the lines within the space. Occasionally a small animal or insect appears under a lip or on the edge of the foot of a vase, but for the most part the designs are abstract, dominated by striped spirals, ovoids and occasional dentate patterns.

31 Each of the spectacular painted pots found at Ban Chiang represents an aesthetic response to form on the part of the painter.

In Thailand the production of bronze artefacts continued after the introduction of iron in the middle to late part of the first millennium BC, and indeed the most sophisticated and elaborate bronze items date from this period. Excavations at Ban Don Ta Phet revealed richly decorated bowls in bronze [33], the latter showing for the first time representations of human life in two-dimensional form. There were also fine examples of jewelry at this site, close to the sea route to India. Evidence of contact with India is furnished by a fine carnelian statuette of a lion, possibly a reference to the Buddha, who at that time was rarely represented in human form. The presence of a double-headed animal pendant made of jade [32] also links this site with cultures overseas. Similar items have been found in contemporary sites in the Philippines and in Sa Huynh sites along the southern Vietnamese coast.

By this time techniques of production had diversified and many artisans had clearly achieved a high level of craftsmanship. The bronze bowls seem to have been cast by means of the lost wax method and then turned on a lathe, reducing the thickness of their bodies to a fine skin. Intricate designs were then worked on the outer surfaces, showing scenes with human figures and animals, flowers and possibly houses. Very similar bowls have been found in India, so it seems that some were made for export. Another technique to appear first during this period is etching. Among the thousands of beads found at the site, many were made of jade, patterned using caustic soda. The technique may have been introduced from India, where it was used with some skill at this time, around the fourth century BC.

Another Iron Age community, at Noen U-Loke, buried its dead with large numbers of bronze ornaments including finger rings, toe rings, belts, bangles and a wonderful spiral head

32 Jade double-headed animal ornament from the Iron Age site at Ban Don Ta Phet discovered in 1975. Almost identical items are found in Iron Age sites in the Philippines and on the Vietnamese coast.

33 Incised frieze on the outside of a bronze bowl from Ban Don Ta Phet. Face and hair 27 mm wide.

ornament, demonstrating the high degree of skill of the artist. One man was buried with seventy-five bronze bangles on each arm, three bronze belts and silver earcoils covered in gold foil. Gold was by this time an important material; one burial contained a large number of gold beads [36], each skilfully fashioned with eight facets.

It was in what is now Vietnam, however, that Bronze Age artists produced their most spectacular work. The village of Dong Son in the Red River delta was first excavated in the 1920s. Since then, archaeologists have applied its name to sites exhibiting the same cultural characteristics, though the village of Dong Son itself was probably not central in political terms. Bronze working had probably been practised in Vietnam since the fourteenth century BC, but during the early part of the period this was limited to tools and ornaments for local use. By the middle of the first millennium BC, iron objects were also being manufactured, and bronze working was reaching a high level of sophistication. Many of the articles produced were highly ornamented ritual objects such as drums, gongs, vessels and weapons. Some of the gongs, usually referred to as drums, are linked stylistically to drums made in Yunnan in southwest China. However, there is a distinct type whose major centre of manufacture was in north Vietnam but which has been found throughout Southeast Asia, with the

34 Detail from tympanum of bronze Dong Son drum from Trong Dong Ngoc Lu, Vietnam.

exception only of Borneo, the Philippines and northeastern
Indonesia. The bronze drums of Southeast Asia were studied by
Franz Heger, an Austrian scholar whose name has been given to
the typology by which they are classified into periods. The oldest
type, Heger I drums, have been found across a wide area of
Southeast Asia stretching along the Sunda chain of islands from
Sumatra to New Guinea. These early examples were cast in one
piece, a considerable technological achievement, with a flat
tympanum and sides that narrow at the 'waist' [37]. The largest can
weigh as much as 100 kilograms and reach to a metre in height.

The original function of the drums is likely to have been
connected with both ritual and rank, with many found buried in
the graves of high status individuals. The materials with which they
were made and the skills needed to manufacture them were such
that only the wealthy would have been able to own them. The
decoration shows considerable variety. The tympana [35] are
generally embellished with regular formal patterns such as
meanders and spirals in circular bands. Between these there are
always bands with flying birds, which may be either herons or
phoenixes. The geometric and repeated figures appear in low
relief [34], having been impressed into the wax using moulds
before the bronze was cast. On the sides of the drums, scenes

35 Tympanum of bronze Dong Son
drum from Trong Dong Ngoc Lu,
Vietnam.

depicting ships or houses peopled with feathered men were incised in the wax by hand. These figurative scenes contain rich detail, though the feathered men who can be identified quite clearly as warriors, dancers or musicians in some examples are so sketchy and indistinct in others that they can no longer be read as human forms.

Dong Son was not the only site of bronze working in this period, nor were drums its only product. Other bronze articles recovered from Dong Son sites include tools and arrowheads, bracelets, bowls and daggers with hilts in the shape of standing human figures. There is also a considerable amount of material associated with this period and culture found in other parts of the region, including a number of sites in the islands. In island Southeast Asia, the Bronze Age had started much later than on the mainland, probably between 500 and 200 BC. Iron and copper technology arrived at about the same time as the introduction of bronze, possibly as a result of contact with northern Vietnam. By the first part of the first millennium BC, bronze was being produced in some quantity in Java and Bali, and perhaps elsewhere. The products of these industries were remarkable in the quality of their design and the skill of their manufacture. The

36 Gold beads found in a grave at Noen U-Loke dating from around AD 250. Each is about 4 mm across.

extraordinary ceremonial bronze axes found in Roti in 1875 may well have been made locally as their style and shape differ considerably from those made in Java [38]. There may be an echo of the Dong Son feathered warriors in the figure represented in low relief on the side of one blade, with a huge ceremonial headdress. A fine axe from Tuban in Java is decorated with a bird of prey carrying a similar axe in its talons, although in shape and design the axe itself is quite different from those from Roti. A further design is shown in a great ornamented socketed axe from Macassar. Another group of objects that date from the Bronze–Iron Age is that of the large bronze flask-shaped vessels found in the islands in Madura, Lampung and Kerinci in Central Sumatra. A similar vessel was found in Kandal, in Cambodia, and it has been suggested that the style may have been inspired by Dong Son bronzes. The flasks, decorated with large bold spiral shapes and triangles, are similar in decorative design to a group of clapperless bells [39], one found in Battambang in Cambodia and four in parts of peninsular Malaysia. It seems likely that these items all originated from the same bronze-casting centre, arriving at their destinations through trade or tribute. By the time of their manufacture, however, bronze production centres had developed in several parts of the region and it is by no means certain that northern Vietnam was their place of origin.

Evidence of local bronze drum manufacture was discovered in Bali, where indented moulds were found, which would produce designs in relief, standing out on the surface; one of these

37 Bronze Dong Son drum from Trong Dong Ngoc Lu, Vietnam. Height 630 mm.

corresponds to the heart-shaped human face that appears on the side of a drum found in Pejeng in Bali. The Bali drums differ technically from the Heger I drums, being cast in two pieces by the lost wax method. Their shape also differs, in that they are taller and more slender, with large handles on the sides, between which the faces on the Pejeng drum appear in pairs.

Some of the most visually striking Prehistoric art in Southeast Asia cannot yet be precisely dated, though it appears to come from the early centuries of this era. It includes a large number of paintings on the walls of caves and tombs, at both mainland and island sites. In Thailand, most figures are painted in red ochre. The scenes include humans and animals, often in what appears to be a representation of a hunt, some with dogs and bows and arrows. Deer, elephants and cattle are among the animals shown in the paintings at Pha Thaem in the northeast of the country [20], which may depict rice cultivation. Dolphins and fish also appear in some of the paintings. Most figures are drawn as silhouettes, with the shapes filled in with flat colour, though there are depictions in 'X-ray' style of a man with a bull at Khao Plara in Thai Thani province. At Tham Pha Daeng, the human figures seem to be wearing skirt cloths, a feather waist ornament and feathery headdresses that recall the figures on the sides of the Dong Son drums. At Tham Ta Duang, a group in procession is carrying what appears to be a large circular drum. Some of these paintings seem to contain a narrative element, though what relationship, if any, there is between these early rock paintings and the murals that appear in temples several centuries later is unclear. They do suggest, however, that the art of wall painting, if introduced to the region from outside, was not an entirely new phenomenon.

In maritime Southeast Asia, cave paintings have been found at a number of sites. Some of the most famous are those at the

38 Bronze ceremonial axe from Savu, eastern Indonesia.

MacCluer gulf on the west coast of New Guinea, while others have been found in Sulawesi, Ceram, the Kei Islands and in Borneo. In Sarawak, the paintings on the wall of one of the Niah caves, first excavated during the period 1954–62, appear to have been associated with death rituals. In front of the red ochre paintings, which depict dancing figures alongside boats, were several coffins in the shape of boats, in which were human remains.

39 Bronze bell from the Dong Son period, found in Malaysia.

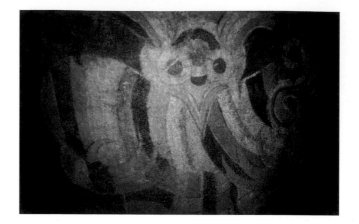

Spectacular paintings in a style unique to Southeast Asia occur in some of the slab-lined burial chambers found in the Pagaralam area of the Pasemah highlands of South Sumatra [40]. The lining of graves with stone slabs does occur elsewhere: such constructions have been found in eastern Taiwan, where they appear to date from 1500 to 800 BC or even earlier. Slab graves also occur in parts of Java and in southern Bali, in both cases associated with bronze items and with objects traded from India such as carnelian beads. The tombs in Pasemah contained items suggesting that they date from the period between the middle of the first century BC and the middle of the first century AD. The chief interest of the Sumatran examples, however, is the multicoloured paintings of human and animal figures, which could possibly have been added at a later date, though this is unlikely. They are made up of zoned areas coloured with red and yellow clay, charcoal and haematite. Two represent a man and buffalo, one appears to show a man with an elephant and another depicts a large bird, possibly an owl. They differ remarkably in style from other paintings found in the region in the complete elision of the distinction between foreground and background, the shapes of the design elements being formed of tessellating pieces like parts of a huge mosaic. The preference for silhouette and profile found elsewhere is also absent: the image of the bird turns face-on to the viewer with the eyes, beak and ear tufts dominating, while below the wings great claws curve up toward the centre of the image. The whole painting is startlingly impressionistic, depicting for the first time in Southeast Asian art what the eye might catch from a glimpse of the subject in reality rather than the artist's understanding of its make-up. The bird's legs are so unimportant as to be barely indicated at all, while the

40 Painting in black ochre, yellow and white on the wall of a chamber grave at Kotaraya Lembak, Pasemah, South Sumatra. Height approx. 1500 mm.

41 Stone sculpture, Pasemah plateau, South Sumatra.

42 Stone sculptures, Pasemah plateau, South Sumatra.

41

talons, completely displaced from them, appear as if at the end of arms, grasping toward their prey. The whole expresses the violence of the creature rather than the elements of it actual form.

The subject matter of the Pasemah paintings seems to relate directly to the stone sculptures also found on the plateau [41, 42]. There are a large number of these, representing human and animal figures in vigorous interaction. Some show men struggling with a snake or an elephant, some show people riding on elephants or buffalo, one is of tigers copulating. There are groups of humans, some including children, as well as single individuals. In one sculpture, depicting two riders on an elephant, there are what appear to be two bronze drums of the Heger I type; the weapons depicted in the sculptures also resemble those excavated in northern Vietnam, thus linking them with the Dong Son era. These sculptures do not seem to be a transformation of wooden sculptures into stone form; many follow closely the shape of the original boulder from which they were cut, with details in relief but sculpted on all sides of the surface. Their dynamism contrasts starkly with the static style of the ancestor figures that were still being carved from wood by some peoples of island Southeast Asia in the twentieth century, and which will be considered in the next chapter. The vigour and energy with which the statues are imbued and the bold, strong modelling of the features and limbs, their twisting and thrusting movements captured in stone, give an effect of power that testifies to the skill of the artists. Perhaps they represent local legendary giants, demons and heroes such as Lidah Pahit (Bitter Tongue) and Mata Empat (Four Eyes) whose rivalry ended when they were turned to stone, or perhaps it was the sculptures that gave rise to the stories. What is certain is that these works contain no hint of Hindu or Chinese influence. While some have suggested that the elephant riders must reflect the effects of Indian culture on the Sumatran population, the style of the sculptures indicates no such influence.

Stone sculptures that may also date from this early period occur in other parts of island Southeast Asia. The most notable are probably the stone figures from the Bada valley in South Sulawesi [43], which seem to be associated with stone burial jars. As is the case with some of the Pasemah statues, the features have been carved in low relief, but in the Bada valley examples these are very rudimentary. The faces are indicated by stylized eyes and nose, often with no mouth, and single lines suggesting the curve of the arm towards the genitalia, which are exaggerated in comparison. In Kalimantan and in Nias there are roughly similar

43 Stone figure, Bada valley. Megaliths in various forms are scattered across the Bada, Napau and Besoa valleys of Central Sulawesi.

images carved in wood, and it may be that in this case there was a transference of the form from wood to stone.

Whatever the dates of these bronze items, wall paintings and stone sculptures, it is clear that by the early centuries of the first millennium AD, artists and craftsmen working in local styles were already proficient in a range of media and were able to express ideas in a range of forms. The arrival of world religions from overseas in the centuries that followed would affect subjects, styles and iconography, but this would take place within an already flourishing and vibrant artistic world.

Chapter 2   Indigenous themes

In contemporary Southeast Asia, many art forms persist that resemble quite closely those produced by some of the earliest inhabitants of the region. While it is true that nowhere does life remain exactly as it was centuries ago, in some places conceptions of the universe and humanity's place within it have retained many elements from protohistoric times. These predate the introduction into the region of Hinduism, Buddhism and other systems of thought that later transformed much artistic expression, especially among the elite. In such places, artists may still use materials and techniques and produce artefacts in shapes and styles similar to those made by their forbears before written records began.

The groups whose material culture is generally supposed to be closest to that of the early settlers in the region are those whose homelands lie beyond the wet-rice growing areas. On the mainland wet rice is grown for the most part in the lowland plains, and in the archipelago on the islands of Java and Bali. Elsewhere, groups such as the Toraja, the Iban, the Ifugao and the Batak, and some islanders such as those of Mentawai, Nias and islands in the southeast of the Indonesian archipelago have traditionally lived in small-scale societies, and their artistic expression seems to retain many ancestral characteristics. On the mainland, some of the peoples of the central highlands of Vietnam fall into this category, as do several in the mountainous north. Some rejected the values of outsiders, while others living in the remote hills or with few products to trade had little contact with them. The symbolic power of their material culture is, however, the most likely reason for its endurance. Even in recent years, when external forces have impinged more than ever on life in Southeast Asia, there seems to have been a remarkable persistence of such cultural forms.

The type of patterning that appears in traditional art has much in common throughout Southeast Asia, with spirals, meanders,

44 Figure of hornbill, *kenyalang*, Iban, Sarawak. Height 800 mm.

zigzags and other geometrical devices prevalent. Many reasons for the similarities have been suggested. Now largely discredited are diffusionist theories which suggested that complexes of motifs and design arrangements were transplanted by invading cultures, usually cultures regarded as superior. Thus the resemblance between some of the patterns on Dong Son drums imported from north Vietnam and those found in carvings and textiles elsewhere is not now seen as evidence of the arrival of a 'Dong Son cultural complex'. Some of these motifs may well have been copied; there is ample evidence of decorative elements borrowed from any number of sources in almost all the ornamental arts. But in fact the evidence suggests that indigenous artists create their own motifs, or select from elsewhere only those elements that resonate with their own culture. Influences almost certainly crossed between cultures within the region itself as much as between the region and cultures beyond it. Similarities of motif could result from any one of these creative interactions, or from a combination of them.

A cosmological belief system based on a tripartite conception of the universe is a recurrent theme among the 'traditional' cultures of Southeast Asia. Often the world is thought of as resting on the back of a vast creature, sometimes a serpent,

Art in traditional societies has a variety of roles, but its chief use relates to the need to make contact with the unseen world, the dwelling place of the spirits of ancestors, deities and other supernatural beings. In addition, and in many ways in association with this, art is used to cement alliances between families and to assert status, rank or political power, as well as enhancing the aesthetic appearance and potency of the environment in which people live. The design and production of a particular type of object may be carried out in accordance with requirements set down by respected authority figures from the past, and deviation from these practices may be thought to reduce the object's power or effectiveness. But this is not to say that there is no innovation. The patterns set down will determine only some aspects of the final version. In every example in every medium the articulation differs slightly, and an examination of individual textiles, sculptures and house forms, for example, will reveal the creative interpretations of individual artists working within the prescribed cultural framework. The Iban weaver who ties motifs into the undyed warp of a cloth she is weaving [45] is not making a mere reproduction but an individual piece of work which will carry its own force, dependent on the skill and knowledge of the maker.

A cosmological belief system based on a tripartite conception of the universe is a recurrent theme among the 'traditional' cultures of Southeast Asia. Often the world is thought of as resting on the back of a vast creature, sometimes a serpent, sometimes a turtle, whose restless shifting may cause turbulence in the ocean or tremors in the earth. Below the earth and in the depths of the sea are spirits who may be malevolent if disturbed, and may even claim the lives of transgressors in the human world. Invisible spirits abound in the natural world, in rocks, streams, trees and pools. Many of the creatures in the fields and forest are spirits that have taken on the shapes of animals. Above the world of humans, the heavens too are inhabited by spirits who may be benevolent or malign, and who can exert a degree of control over the lives of humans. Some may be founding deities, some beings associated with the elements, and some may be linked with disease. Others may be the spirits of ancestors, often made manifest in the shape of animals or birds. By appeasing those spirits who have been angered or by seeking help from those whose assistance can be obtained, villagers can avert danger or bad fortune, or ensure success in hunting or a plentiful harvest. Much creative energy and care is given to making contact with such beings, through the design of offerings themselves, of implements for use in their making, or to otherwise arranging aspects of the material world to please them. In many societies, what is deemed important is the maintenance of balance through acting in harmony with natural laws; lessons drawn from nature may govern the rules of behaviour. Transgressing such rules affects the community by making it 'hot', and purifying rituals may have to be undertaken to restore the desired 'cool' environment. These ideas about the structuring of the cosmological and social worlds and their relationship with flora, fauna and other elements of nature find expression in many of the cultures of Southeast Asia, especially in the upland areas, the forest interiors and the eastern islands of the archipelago.

In artistic representations of the tripartite universe, the upper world is often symbolized in visual form by birds. As well as the herons engraved on early bronze drums, the hornbill appears, engraved as a figurehead on the stern of a ship. The giant hornbill [44], a large bird with a distinctive casque behind its bill, continues to be a central feature in many island cultures. In Mentawai, hornbill figures play a part in ritual. In Sarawak, carved representations of hornbills are placed on high posts and displayed at the hornbill feast in honour of Singalang Burong, the god of heaven, who manifests as a kite but is represented as a hornbill. These hornbill figures, or *kenyalang*, are said by some to be representative of this creator god, while others consider them to stand for human ancestors. In all cases, however, they are

associated with the upper realm. The lower world tends to be indicated by underwater creatures such as crocodiles, shrimp, squid and fish of various kinds. One central image is that of the *naga*, or sea serpent, which was thought by some groups to control the four cardinal points. The scales of the naga as well as those of pythons and fish have symbolic resonance in artistic representations throughout the region. In Sumba cloths, they are said to relate to the idea of rebirth. Snakes, which shed their skin, are particularly associated with regeneration, and in Kodi, in West Sumba, some of the *ikat* cloths bear the names of snakes.

Linking the upper realm with the lower, the sky with the earth, is the image of the tree, interpreted in different ways in different parts of the region. Among the Barito peoples of southern Borneo, the role of the tree in uniting the two domains is explicit, the roots being connected with the lower world and the upper branches with the world above. A huge wooden post [46] embellished with carvings of a dragon, representing the female lower world, and a hornbill, symbolizing the male upper world, is erected at funerals. The union of male and female, the origin of life itself, is represented in this image of a tree. However, not all trees

45 Iban weavers often base their designs on dreams, as with this *pua kumbu*, entitled 'Kelekuh Ambun Belabuh'. Upper Rejang river, Sarawak, early 20th century. 2652 × 1550 mm.

46 Kenyah ritual post, *belawing*, with hornbill and dragon. Datah Bilang, Middle Mahakam River, East Kalimantan.

have the same metaphorical force. Accounts of the art of Southeast Asia refer frequently to the 'tree of life', a term accurately applicable only where the tree has connotations of fertility, life or prosperity. References to particular trees also vary in meaning, with the *rengas* and *aro* trees, for example, being associated with supernatural spirits in Central Sumatra. It is not clear whether or not the tree images prevalent in Lampung textiles carry associations of fertility.

The automatic interpretation of ship images as 'ships of death' is similarly suspect. It is widely believed that the souls of the departed migrate to their place of origin after death, but while images of ships are widespread, especially in island Southeast Asia, they may have several referents. Some are clearly connected with death: for example, the remains of high-ranking Batak individuals were deposited in stone sarcophagi that were often made in the shape of boats. But legends of the arrival of founding ancestors by sea, either from the north or the west, occur in many societies, and houses built in the shape of ships are often said to relate to this rather than to notions concerning the journeys of the dead. On the island of Savu, both the island itself and the houses built there may be conceived metaphorically as ships. The gable ends of houses in many parts of the region are referred to as 'sails' and some have a 'prow' and a 'stern' end. However, boat imagery occurs in a much wider range of contexts and the suggestion that such houses are symbols of the arrival of ancient forebears has largely been discredited.

47 Ngaju Dayak 'ships of the dead' are part of the funeral furnishing. The boat coffin, death house and tree of life are accompanied by an orchestra. The Ngaju believe that the soul journeys in such a boat to the next world. Replica made of rubber latex. 240 × 465 mm.

48 This design of a ship carrying horses, riders and standing figures, with fish in the water and birds above, features often on cotton ceremonial cloths from southern Sumatra. These cloths were used especially in marriage rituals, often forming part of the gift exchange between the lineages of bride and groom. *Tampan*, Lampung region, Sumatra. Supplementary weft. 870 × 760 mm.

The top of the sheath of the keris, a type of dagger that is an icon of both Malay and Javanese identity, is often carved in the shape of a ship's hull. Cloths with a ship design in Lampung are used chiefly at marriage ceremonies, where they may refer to the journey through life on which the couple are embarking [48]. Thus ship imagery relates not just to death but to a whole range of situations, often transitional and ceremonial stages in the life cycle [47].

The role of ancestors is key in the art of small-scale societies, many of which can trace their genealogical origins back to their founders. Often one or more of the founders is thought to have descended from the upper world; some groups refer to a union between a male and female figure, one relating to the earth, the other to the sky. Others recount legends of the arrival of one or all of their forbears by ship from a foreign land. Where descent from the originators is key to a claim to ancestral land or privilege, their memory is often kept alive and their goodwill secured through making and using sculptures which may be commemorative or which may act as receptacles for each spirit when invoked.

In the highlands of Sulawesi, both the Mamasa and the Sa'dan Toraja make carved effigies of human figures in association with death rituals. The *tau-tau* effigies of the Mamasa represent the deceased and are symbolically brought to life by their makers [50]. The tau-tau is dressed in the costume of a high-ranking noble before 'dying' in a ceremony performed by the maker, which enables the soul of the deceased to pass on to the abode of the dead. The Sa'dan Toraja place their dead of high rank in vaults or rock chambers in the cliffs for a time, with the tau-tau in front, standing as guardians overlooking the fields. These tau-tau figures are portraits, much more so than any other ancestor figure in Southeast Asia. They continue to be cared for, for example by the changing of their clothing, long after the burial of the remains.

Sculptures of ancestors show remarkable similarities across the region. The squatting figures found in Borneo closely resemble others found in Flores and Sumatra. However, not all sculpted figures represent ancestors. The figures that were placed around the tombs in a Jorai village in Vietnam probably represented followers, possibly slaves, who were to accompany the deceased on his journey to the next world, where they would minister to his needs. Many of the figures found in public places at the centre of villages in parts of southern Maluku, on the other hand, are thought to have represented village founders. In this society figures of more recently deceased relatives, both male and female, were kept within the house, often on intricately carved altars. That these carvings represent individuals of high status is clear from the heirloom jewelry they wear and the seats on which they are installed; the variety of detail in the features and posture suggests that many are in a sense portraits. In the *adu zatua* ancestor figures of Nias, on the other hand, rank rather than the individual was emphasized in the carving [49]. When an elder died

49 Carved wooden ancestor figure, *adu zatua*, Nias. Height 242 mm.

an image of him would be placed inside the house attached to a post or fixed to the wall where he could be called upon for protection at times of crisis, or guidance at celebrations such as a wedding or the birth of a child. Tall forked or feathered headdresses indicated high rank, while small unpolished figures might represent deceased infants or individuals of low status. The influence of missionaries in the nineteenth century led to the removal and destruction of many of these carvings of ancestors, and their original function and meaning have been lost.

Despite the variety of contexts in which ancestor figures function, they seem always to relate to the sense of the presence of the dead among the living and to a need to influence their spirits during and after transition to the next world. They appear both in societies that trace their descent along the male line and in those where both male and female lines are considered (in which individuals can belong to two separate descent groups). In the Ngada region of Flores, each matrilineal village traditionally contained at its centre two ancestral shrines, one honouring a

50 Mortuary effigies (tau-tau), Tana Toraja, Sulawesi.

51 Pillar of ngadhu, Ngada region, Flores. The ngadhu post is topped by a conical thatched roof and surrounded with stones at its base.

52 Forked *peo* post made of *hebu* wood, Ngada region, Flores. One of the symbols on the post represents a *taka*, a pendant In double axe-head shape which is used in Flores as part of the bridewealth. The motif closely resembles the form of the *marangga* of West Sumba (see 54) though a *taka* pendant is about one third the size of a *marangga*.

female, the other a male ancestor. The female shrine had to be built first, and consisted of a small house, rectangular in shape. In some areas the entrances were provided with boards carved with elaborate designs, and figures of male and female riders on horseback often guarded the entrance. The male shrine was a *ngadhu* post, carved in tripartite form symbolizing the three components of *adat* costume: the headcloth, the wide sash worn across the chest, and the waist cloth [51]. In patrilineal villages, instead of a ngadhu there is a forked *peo* post [52], embellished with symbols representing the sun, moon, the clans and the double-axe, or *taka*, a female symbol.

The balance between male and female worlds lies at the core of representation in Indonesian cultures. One aspect of this is in the division of labour: men are responsible for working wood and metal, women for textiles, mats and much basketry. A similar division is revealed in the reciprocal exchanges made between the families of bride and groom at a marriage in most traditional societies. Among the items expected from the groom's family are variously weapons, ivory, metal earrings and other jewelry, cattle

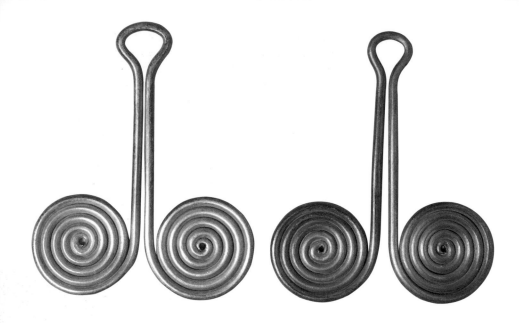

or horses, whereas the central gift from the bride's side is likely to be textiles. In Batak society, the generic names given to these gifts indicate the type of goods deemed appropriate: gifts from the man's side are called *piso* (literally, knife), whereas those from the woman's side are called *ulos* (textiles), though they may include other items besides knives and cloths. This opposition may relate to a further symbolic opposition between fertility, represented by the textile, the product of the life-giving creative forces of the woman, and death, represented by the weapon with which men kill to provide meat or to procure the heads of enemies. Among the Iban, part of the preparations for dyeing the yarn used for weaving is known as 'the woman's warpath', making the conceptual opposition explicit. This opposition is at the same time expressive of complementarity, since both men and women could be said to contribute fertility to the community, one by giving birth and the other by bringing life force in the form of slaughtered animals and, in the past, the heads of enemies. Art can operate as an expression of such polarities but also of reconciliation between them [53], especially where male and female imagery are combined in one object.

In the art of Sumba, grave stelae may be decorated with a range of images, including iconographic references to the lineage, wealth and degree of ritual precedence of the deceased [54]. Lineage is normally signified in an extended botanical metaphor, in which descendants are regarded as the fruits and flowers or

53 Spiral forms appear frequently in North Sumatran designs. Here they are shaped into ear pendants, *padung-padung*, made of thick folded silver wire. Karo Batak women wore them partially supported by their headdresses, one pointing forwards and one backwards, symbolizing the shifting power relations between a husband and wife in marriage. 80 × 64 mm.

sprouts and shoots of their ancestral line. Rank may be indicated by a totemic image such as a turtle, which is associated with one of the noble lineages in Sumba. An image frequently used to indicate wealth is that of the *mamuli* earring, one of the items given as bridewealth by a Sumbanese groom. The cavity-like mamuli shape appears frequently in the arts of Sumba, closely connected as it is with ideas of female procreativity. On grave stelae, it is usually surrounded by male imagery, often of creatures such as the rooster, the male goat or the stallion with its tail erect. In the same way, skirt cloths woven by and for women often include a male image, the skull tree, whereas the male *hinggi* shoulder cloths, which may also bear male imagery, sometimes feature female symbols such as the mamuli.

54 The tombstone of the Raja of Anakalang in West Sumba is dominated by the figures of a male and female; other smaller figures appear on the sides. Among the geometric designs decorating the niche in which they stand is the *marangga* motif, which represents a pectoral.

The patterning of the hinggi cloths of East Sumba [56] has been analyzed in depth by Marie Jeanne Adams, who remarked on how its structural properties appear to represent a transformation of social structures. The motifs are arranged in horizontal bands symmetrically placed on either side of a central horizontal band. In addition, the design is usually symmetrical about the vertical axis, and more often than not the motifs themselves are arranged in facing pairs. Adams argues that the meeting of the bands at the centre and the motifs with one another corresponds to the structure of the traditional village, in which the opposing rows of houses of warrior clans are divided by a mediating row of houses belonging to members of the priestly class. This visual trope of almost-symmetry, of balance and mediation, is prevalent in visual arrangements in many media in Southeast Asia, but is perhaps most striking in textiles. Many of the cloths woven in Indonesia are made up of three horizontal bands set across three vertical bands, which may either be woven separately, or divided by colour. In a Batak *ulos ni tondi*, or 'soul cloth', given to a woman during her first pregnancy by her mother, the two ends are specifically referred to as 'male' and 'female', with the difference

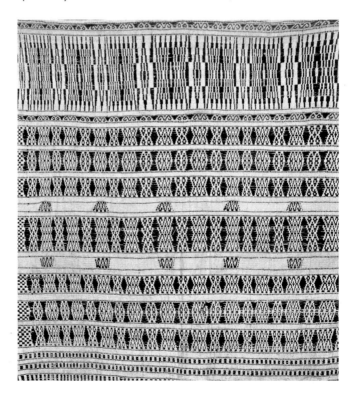

55 *Pinar halak* panel on a Batak '*ulos ni tondi*', or soul cloth. Each end of such cloths has a panel, one female, one male, into which patterns relating to the life of the wearer are woven. Lake Toba, North Sumatra. Panel 470 × 420 mm.

56 The mirroring of the images on this *hinggi* cloth, as well as the groupings of design motifs, seem to reflect similar patterns in aspects of the society of East Sumba. Man's mantle with dominant squid motif, Sumba, Indonesia. 2860 × 1200 mm.

indicated in the patterning of the *pinar halak* [55], the panels woven in supplementary weft at each end of the cloth. A tripartite arrangement occurs also in many of the traditional textiles of the mainland, such as the skirt cloths of the Karen and other neighbouring groups. The ship cloths of Lampung often exhibit what appears at first glance to be symmetry; on closer examination small deviations in the detail become evident. In the binakol blankets of Luzon, slight irregularities in the patterning are said to allow a medium who has entered trance through the dazzling pattern of the cloth to find a way out and return to the everyday world. Symmetry is also sometimes manifested in the perceived relationship between human and non-human worlds. The Iban of Sarawak [57], for example, have been reported as imagining that the 'souls' of rice plants inhabit a world very much like our own, but in mirror image. Similarly, the Kayan and Kenyah of Borneo are said to conceive of the next world as a reverse of the world of the living, where the black patterning of tattoos that cover a woman's skin will shine white, allowing her spirit to find its way.

Art can be used as a means of penetrating the spirit world in various ways. One is through masks [58], which allow the wearer to take on the identity or be infused with the spirit of another being, be it an animal, demon or ancestor spirit. This occurs especially at festivals held to repel malevolent forces, which may attack a community in several ways, including the devouring of life force. The souls of the departed, if not properly laid to rest, may also pose a threat unless their potential for harm is removed by exorcism. In many of the cultural groups in Borneo, dancers act out their alliance with the god by dressing as guardian demons,

57 Rattan mat, Iban, from the upper Rejang river in Sarawak. The design is referred to as 'remau' (tiger) though the representation is symbolic rather than visual. The designs closely resemble those used by neighbouring Kenyah/Kayan peoples. Maker: Gading anak Mayau. 3085 × 1305 mm.

58 Ritual mask of the Jorai people, Central Vietnam. Height 390 mm.

scaring evil spirits and villagers alike, or as benevolent supernatural beings bringing blessings from the upper world. Masks are also worn in re-enactments of myths; the wild boar mask worn by Kenyah and Kayan men is part of a ritual that recreates the introduction of rice seed by outsiders [59]. Faces appear also as protective motifs on all kinds of object, from monuments commemorating the dead to carriers for infants. These *hudo,* or monster faces, are characterized by bulging eyes and bared fangs, often accompanied by horns and protruding tongues. Some masks, in Borneo and elsewhere, depict alien forces of the human kind. The masks once used at festivals amongst the Jorai of Vietnam seem to represent bearded men, foreign visitors from the human world rather than from the upper or lower realms.

House forms, too, show similarities across the region that seem to reflect a heritage that is to a considerable degree a shared one. The houses depicted in the decorative panels on the drums of Dong Son show the characteristic combination of piles or pillars supporting a large saddle roof [60]. This type of structure is still widespread in the region and almost certainly predates the

59 Wild boar mask, *hudo' urung babui,* worn at the rice-sowing festival. Upper Mahakam river, East Kalimantan. Height 420 mm.

60 Traditional house, Tana Toraja, Sulawesi.

Bronze Age. While there are sound functional advantages to the design, its persistence probably also results from aesthetic and symbolic satisfactions. In particular, the three-tiered division of space accords with deeply held notions about the world, both social and cosmological. The space below the house is used for animals, the space within for humans, while the loft area often contains ancestral items, more closely associated with the world of the spirits. House-building rituals appear to confirm this interpretation: in parts of Sumatra, sweet offerings such as sugar cane and honey are hung in the rafters for spirits of the air, and powerful talismanic items such as iron, dung and putrefied eggs placed in the ground to repel earth demons. In south Nias, the pillars of the house are said to represent the legs of an ancestor, while the façade and roof represent his face and crown respectively. The three-tiered division also often operates in relation to the floor levels, for example the typical vernacular Malay house has a low verandah at the front rising to an inner entrance hall, with the house core, the living area, a further step up.

The materials from which a house is built must be appropriate not just in terms of durability, enabling it to withstand the deleterious effects of heat, rain, flood and insects, but also in spiritual terms. In cultural groups where every part of nature is believed to be animated by vital force – *semangat* in Malay, but with various names in other places – the house carries with it the forces contained within the materials from which it is made, which are renewed when the house becomes an entity in itself. To the extent that humans have played a part in its construction, their efforts too are transmitted to the house. This is perhaps especially true of the carved and painted decorations that embellish the exterior and sometimes the interior. Talismanic forms are depicted especially over doorways and window frames, through which malignant spirits might otherwise enter. A common feature of such designs is continuity of line, a phenomenon that bears a special power, and of which the epitome is the 'endless knot' that

61 Endless-knot carving from Kupang, Timor. Such knots occur also in Chinese and Islamic art, where they carry talismanic significance.

62 Woman's tubeskirt, *ei*, made
from handspun cotton and natural
dyes, from the Lesser Blossom
group in Savu, eastern Indonesia.
The Ledo motif in the main ikat
panel refers to an ancestress.
1400 × 545 mm.

appears on many traditional houses [61]. It finds a correspondence in the completed loops of ritual textiles from Bali, Lombok and other parts of the region, whose continuous warp embodies the force contained in the life cycle and only released when the warps are cut. In Bali, when the warps of the double-ikat *gringsing* cloth have been cut, its symbolic force is spent and the textile discarded.

The dimensions of a house may be determined by a need for symbolic congruity with the dimensions of its inhabitants. Among Malays, the distance between house posts was traditionally determined by the arm-span of the woman whose house it was to be. The same is true of the dagger, or keris – its dimensions must correspond to the finger widths of the person who will own it. Not only must the measurements be appropriate, but there must be a correspondence in the character of owner and weapon. A mismatch might mean a dangerous clash causing harm to the owner or to a third party by his hand. This idea that an object has a kind of 'essence' deriving from the materials from which it is made and the methods and formulae of its manufacture lies at the core of artistic production in Southeast Asia.

One aspect of such formulae is number, which plays an important part in aesthetics. Of prime importance is the avoidance of even numbers and a preference for the odd. In traditional houses in Jambi, for example, there must be an odd number of rafters in the roof and rungs on the ladder leading to the entrance. It has been suggested that in Southeast Asia even numbers express a sense of completion akin to lifelessness, whereas odd numbers demand a continuation, signifying dynamism and thus life. Numbers have other significances: in Savu the number of black bands of a woman's ikat skirt traditionally indicated to which of the two matrilineal descent groups on the island the wearer belonged. Traditional sarongs were made of two bands sewn together. If each band contained seven black stripes the wearer was a member of the Greater Blossom group (Hubi Ae), if four the Lesser Blossom group (Hubi Iki) [62]. Numbers are also significant in the formulae for the manufacture of certain objects: the power of a particular keris, for example, may lie partly in the number of sources from which the ore for the metal was obtained. Again, this is likely to be an odd number.

As new relationships have developed between traditional cultures and those in the world beyond, artists have responded in several ways [63]. The introduction of new materials and techniques, access to markets, the development of demand for particular products and changes in perceptions of the nature of the world have all brought modifications to artistic production. In some cases external influences have been absorbed and incorporated into existing forms, resulting in a harmonious melding of style and subject. Some traditional practices have been set aside permanently, others taken up again in a rearticulation of long-standing visual and material expressions. Such changes both reflect and challenge social and political circumstances. Motifs, colours and shapes like those of the hinggi cloths of East Sumba, once the prerogative of chiefs and aristocrats, may now be used by entrepreneurs whose status in the modern world is not determined by lineage. Where religious allegiances have changed, the iconography of the new religion may be intertwined with that of the old, with a concomitant adjustment of meanings in both. Performances once held to contact the spirit world may now be staged for an audience of foreigners, keen to experience an 'authenticity' that is both perpetuated and undermined by their presence. Some lament such changes, seeing them as a loss of valuable heritage, but in fact transformations in artistic expression are part of a long-standing and continuing process, itself a central characteristic of Southeast Asian art.

63 Staffs used by Batak shamans in North Sumatra were already being copied locally to sell to tourists in the 1920s. The unusual shape of this one suggests that it is genuine. Height 1560 mm.

Chapter 3   Hindu visions

Indian culture began to influence that of Southeast Asia around the beginning of the first millennium AD, initially through trade contact. The region by now already possessed a flourishing artistic tradition, with well-developed technological skills and knowledge, and it would not have been difficult for local producers to adopt aspects of Indian material culture and integrate them into their repertoire. One such key feature of Indian culture was religion, including aspects of both Buddhist and Hindu thought and practice, which probably began to arrive in Southeast Asia at around the same time. With the exception of a few small pockets of immigrant communities, Hinduism continues to thrive today only in Bali, and there in a particular form that departs in many ways from the religion as found on the Indian subcontinent. However, ideas, liturgical practices, iconography and artistic forms the roots of which lie in Hinduism are evident in all the countries of the region. Echoes survive in monumental architecture, in the performing arts, in the rituals and paraphernalia of court life and in the characters and legends relating to the Hindu pantheon that have inspired the Southeast Asian imagination for centuries. These

64 Detail of a Javanese batik textile bearing the 'Semeru' design, in which the holy mountain is represented in repeated peaks across the cloth. Stylized forms of Garuda, the mount of Vishnu, also appear.

65 Mandala on a temple ceiling, painted in the nine colours symbolic in Balinese Hinduism, each associated with a deity and direction in the cosmos. Kintamani, Bali.

elements are still very much alive, permeating much of the art of the region despite the relatively small number of followers of Hinduism itself.

The Hindu vision of a world animated by deities, themselves manifestations of the forces that pervade the living world, would have found a ready home in Southeast Asia. Gods who might appear in any one of several manifestations, animal, human or transcendental, probably corresponded in many ways with those supernatural beings who were believed to influence the lives of indigenous people. Hindu gods may have had different names, but their powers and energies were similar. The notion of the absolute, of a creative life force suffusing the universe, was probably a familiar one, even if the terms in which it was expressed were new. The name of the creator god of the old Karo Batak religion, Batara Guru, is derived from Sanskrit, and his role corresponds with that of Shiva. Parallels between the Iban fertility god, Pulang Gana, and Shiva have also been noted, and the title Petara, derived from the Hindu 'Batara' and applied to the high gods in traditional Iban religion, also shows that Hindu ideas have played a part there. Such elements of Hinduism seem to have been absorbed into the religious systems of Southeast Asian peoples by way of a rearticulation rather than a transformation of existing ideas. The iconographic vocabulary of Hinduism also corresponded with some of the existing symbolic motifs.

Fundamental to Hindu influence on art in Southeast Asia is the cosmological conception of the universe with Mount Meru, the abode of the gods, at its centre [64]. The mountain is surrounded by seven oceans and six mountain ranges, beyond which lies the primordial ocean with its four islands, one the dwelling place of humankind. The world of man and the world of the gods is linked by a causeway, manifested in the rainbow. The idea of the cosmic mountain is likely to have resonated with beliefs in mountains and hills as the homes of spirits; such projections from the earth's surface are still today sites of pilgrimage and offerings, especially on the mainland but also in Java and Hinduized Bali, where the great volcanoes are regarded as having a life and spirit of their own. The mountain is a frequent image in the art of all parts of the region, as are mythological beasts, many of which in Hinduism inhabit the forest on the slopes of the sacred mountain and the ranges surrounding it.

The cardinal points were already important in relation to burial practices, and probably also in house building and agriculture, with the position of the sun playing a major part in the

organization and orientation of such activities. The Hindu mandala [65], or cosmic diagram, in which the world is conceived in terms of a sacred centre surrounded by four cardinal points, was readily subsumed into a belief system that already seems to have conceptualized the world in terms of four directions. The Sumatran Kubu conceive of the human and upper worlds as being held together at the four corners, with a deity guarding the integrity of the edges. The association of particular deities, colours, numbers and elements with the cardinal and intermediate points as well as stages in the life cycle, may derive from Indian thought. Aspects of this cosmology have penetrated deep into the consciousness of many peoples of the region who have long since forgotten the core religion that brought it to their shores.

The deities of the Hindu pantheon were adopted in various ways and to differing degrees by local populations. In keeping with a tradition of reverence for high-ranking ancestors, who were believed to become one with the spirit world after death, many local rulers came to be seen, and perhaps promoted themselves, as manifestations or descendants of Hindu deities. Many representations of Hindu deities were regarded in Southeast Asian contexts primarily as images of local kings or queens. Of Brahma, Shiva and Vishnu, the three principal deities of the Hindu pantheon, Shiva was one of the most popular in early times, almost certainly as a result of his association with fertility and, to a lesser extent, the female principle of the moon [66]. In places of worship Shiva was represented by his symbol, the phallic lingam [see also 4], often placed above a yoni, representing the female

66 Carving of Shiva Nataraja, the dancing Shiva, on the pediment of the east entrance to the porch, in front of the main sanctuary of Prasat Phanom Rung, a Khmer stone monument in northeastern Thailand. The dancing Shiva symbolizes both the creation and destruction of the universe.

principle. There were also cults of Vishnu, a god with multiple avatars, or incarnations, including such animal forms as the turtle and the fish. It was his vehicle, the man-eagle Garuda, which has had the most lasting impact on the art of the region. Brahma, the creator god, was never as popular as Vishnu and Shiva, though he appears with his mount, the goose, in early statuary. Indra, the king of the gods, also found favour at one time, especially at the Cambodian court.

In addition to the male gods, references to a plethora of female deities began to appear in the Hindu world from the fifth century onwards. Many of these grew out of the idea of the great goddess Mahadevi, who in one aspect personified the active element of the impersonal absolute. Later she developed many guises, among them the manifestation of the active power of male deities or ideas associated with them such as wealth, earth or fertility. In Indonesia, in the form of Dewi Sri, the rice goddess, she came to symbolize fertility. In Java effigies of Dewi Sri are still made from the first cut stalks of the rice harvest. In Bali the *cili* [67], a stylized female shape that appears in a variety of forms and materials, is often associated with Dewi Sri and fertility in general. Cili figures appear especially on *lamak*, the runners made of palm leaf that decorate altars or shrines and provide a base for offerings. Figures of Dewi Sri in her role as fertility goddess are also made for use at weddings in Java, in the shape of the Loro Blonyo figures of Dewi Sri herself and her consort Dewa Sadono, which are placed in front of the ritual marriage bed.

As well as these core components, many other ideas associated with Hinduism were introduced to Southeast Asia. Some were contained in the *shastra*, sacred Indian treatises which included guidelines relating to architecture, literature, dance and other art forms. These may have been brought in manuscript form by gurus, scholars and priest-architects, or they may have been taught directly to local craftsmen and artists. In addition Southeast Asian scholars studying overseas may well have been introduced to Indian astronomy, which by the fifth century had taken up the trigonometric calculation system of the Greeks and the Romans, and which is very much in evidence in the architectural monuments of Angkor especially.

Archaeological findings suggest that by the first century AD, trading links between polities on the Indian subcontinent and communities along the shores of the mainland and the larger islands had existed for some time. Around this period connections at a political level began; legends suggest that this may

67 A Balinese rice maiden figure representing Dewi Sri, made from straw. c. 1960. Height 410 mm.

sometimes have taken the form of intermarriage between the daughters of local leaders and aristocratic men from India. City states began to flourish along the coasts of Southeast Asia, especially those of present-day Vietnam and down to the Malay Peninsula. Many of these gained their wealth from participating in the trade that was then being conducted between the Roman Empire and India to the west and China to the east. The earliest such polity to be recorded was referred to in third-century Chinese texts as Funan; its authority extended over much of the southern part of present-day Cambodia. Excavations at Oc Eo, thought to be one of the centres of Funan, have uncovered imported items of both Roman and Indian origin as well as objects bearing testimony to the influence of imported faiths – Buddhism as well as Hinduism. Funan is said to have been founded by the

union of an Indian prince, Kaundinya, and a local princess, Soma, a legend that echoes the blending of local tradition with cultural elements from overseas characteristic of Southeast Asian art from this time onward.

The earliest architectural remains of Hinduism in Southeast Asia are the tower-shrines or sanctuary towers, usually built on hilltops. At My Son (in present-day Vietnam) in the kingdom of

68 Shivaite brick shrine, B1, at My Son in Central Vietnam.

Champa, a centre for Hindu worship from as early as the fourth century, the oldest surviving monuments date back to the seventh century. The most important of these buildings were the single-cell shrines, or *kalan* [68], sometimes built in a row of three, in Champa aligned on a north–south axis. Cham towers were constructed mainly in brick, with stone used sparingly for door posts, lintels and some decorative elements. There was little emphasis on the foundations or terraces, but attention was given to the substantial projection at the front, which echoed the shape of the tower itself, and the false doorways on the other faces of the building. On the main body of the building, vertical lines were emphasized, sometimes by means of pilasters or stepped recesses. Above it horizontal mouldings under the stepped roof lent solidity and contributed to the balance and harmony of the structure.

However, it was in their sculpture that Cham artists excelled. Cham sculpture is characterized by the robust volumes of the figures, the limbs proportionally large and solid but softened by smoothly modelled surfaces. The facial features are simple and strong, with fleshy lips, often gently smiling. Jewelry is prominent, especially in the later periods when it comes to dominate the figures; large pedestals on which the statue of a central deity is mounted are also a typical feature. The figures sculpted in high relief on the sides of these pedestals represent some of the greatest achievements of Cham art [70]. Among the most beautiful are the dancers on a sandstone pedestal from Tra Kieu, by the tenth century the main Cham religious centre. An earlier pedestal from a seventh-century temple at My Son supported a brick lingam on a basin, a yoni which acted as a receptacle for the offerings poured over it by devotees in the Hindu *puja* purification ritual. On the riser of the stairway of this pedestal is another group of dancers. The arrangement of these figures illustrates the ability of Cham sculptors to create images of power and balance while representing the anatomically impossible poses necessitated by the technical demands of high relief. The combination of vigour and balance within a squarely controlled framework continued throughout the period of Cham classical art.

Freestanding figures of *dvarapala*, semi-divine guardian figures in dramatic and striking poses, are generally the most vigorous in Cham art. The images of the gods themselves were more highly stylized. Temples to Shiva often housed a lingam in place of a figure of the god himself, but some images of Shiva and of other deities have survived. These tend to be relatively small, and although some earlier examples were sculpted in the round, the

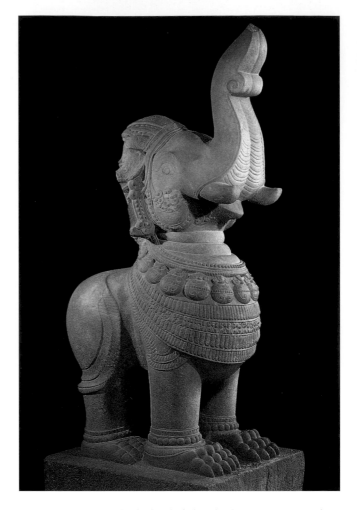

majority were carved in high relief, their backs set against a stele. There was little attempt at realism, with the limbs arranged in conventions derived from Indian representations, but adapted to fit the demands of the medium.

In the later period Cham sculptors depicted animals and mythological beasts, some of which are unique to Cham art [69]. The elephant-lion was probably used as a guardian statue in front of a shrine; it may represent one of the creatures to be found in the forests on the slopes of Mount Meru. A stairway dragon has the so-called Thap Mam motif resembling shells around its neck. Its shape, partly curving back on itself, and carved in strong relief, ends in a slightly off-centre curlicue. Another distinctive element has been named the 'female breast motif', very noticeable in

69 Gajasimha (elephant-lion). Thap Mam style, c. 12th century. Sandstone. Height 2150 mm.

70 Dancer from a pedestal from Tra Kieu, Champa, 10th century. Fine buff sandstone. Height 630 mm.

76

Cham art of the twelfth century. Various reasons have been put forward for its widespread use, though no explanation has been fully accepted by scholars. Already during the eleventh century the Cham empire had begun its decline and by the thirteenth century its art had also become less vibrant, its statuary increasingly static, without the vitality so apparent in the earlier pieces.

Throughout its existence, the kingdom of Champa had close relations with neighbouring states, among them Cambodia, with which it was often in conflict. The site that came to be established as the centre of the Khmer empire and from which Khmer kings exerted power over a region including much of present-day northeastern Thailand, is known as Angkor. Dozens of temples were built at Angkor over a period of several hundred years; the first of these was built in the ninth century by Indravarman, a king who asserted his authority on earth by adopting the name of the king of heaven.

This royal association with one or other of the principal gods of Hinduism was strengthened over the ensuing centuries, so that the king became a symbol of power, fertility and life itself. The idea of the ruler as axis of the universe took root throughout the region; the titles of the later Central Javanese rulers of Yogyakarta and Surakarta, for example, referred to them explicitly as the 'nail' and the 'navel' of the world. Divine power descending from heaven was believed to channel down through the ruler and on outwards in decreasing strength to lesser mortals. Any exercise of this power diminished it, however, and the king was regarded

71 The arrangement of towers in a row of three found in Hindu monuments, such as Preah Ko, also occurs in Buddhist structures. Bat Chum was dedicated in the 10th century to Buddha, Avalokiteshvara and Prajnaparamita.

ideally as the still centre of the kingdom. These ideas found a
harmonious correspondence with the already widespread idea of
a life force that was dissipated through excretions such as sweat
and body heat and even the use of one's voice or casting a shadow.

Indravarman founded a number of buildings that still stand in
the Angkor region, including Preah Ko and Bakong, at Hariharalaya
(present-day Roluoh). Each contains important features
reproduced by later royal builders. One is the sanctuary tower,
probably primarily a place of worship and, in keeping with the
Southeast Asian tradition of reverence for ancestral chiefs, a
memorial to the founder. As with the Cham towers, at Preah Ko
there are three in a row, each one four-sided and with a stepped
roof [71]. The doorways on each of the four sides are elaborately
decorated, particularly the lintel and the pediment above it.
Carved reliefs of guardian figures stand on either side of the
doorways on each side of the tower, again a feature of much of the
monumental architecture of Southeast Asia in the classical period.

The other important feature, clearly evident at Bakong, is that
of the 'temple-mountain', a temple designed to represent a
mountain [72]. At Bakong, a pyramid was constructed consisting of
five stepped platforms at the top of which was the sanctuary
tower containing the lingam, the symbol of the divine power of

72 The Shivaite temple of Bakong
at Angkor. Although the site was
consecrated in 881, much of what
we see now may have been built
much later, which makes the dating
of such monuments particularly
problematic. The central tower
was not built until the 12th century.

the kingdom. The whole complex is contained within four enclosures consisting of moats and walls, with causeways linking the exterior, secular world with the interior, sacred space. The balustrades on the causeway crossing the moat on the east and west sides are formed from the bodies of seven-headed naga, a feature repeated at Angkor Wat and at other Khmer temple sites. The strict alignment of the buildings on an east–west axis exemplifies the rigid adherence in Khmer architecture to geometrical and astronomical rules, which create a strong sense of symmetry and order. Similarly, the pattern of building a central sanctuary on a terrace at the corner of which stand four smaller towers, and of enclosing the temple complex within concentric walls, laid down a model that continued to dominate the design of Khmer monuments, and was echoed in central Java. Other features of Bakong that were to reappear are the four *gopura*, gateways facing the cardinal points and leading to the highest platform on which stands the sandstone sanctuary tower, itself guarded by guardian figures carved into the stone.

The prime example in Cambodia of the temple-mountain concept, however, is the much later temple of Angkor Wat, built by Suryavarman II in the twelfth century, not far from Indravarman's capital [73]. Suryavarman's name associates him with

73 Angkor Wat from the northwest, showing the five main towers and the outer gallery.

Surya, the god of the sun, and the temple itself embodies Hindu themes. Its central tower clearly symbolizes the central peak of Mount Meru, the axis of the universe, and the four supporting towers represent the four surrounding peaks. The walls enclosing the temple symbolize the mountains that edge the world of the gods, and the moat around it the seas beyond.

The symbolism went further. The Khmer city of Angkor Thom, enclosed during the reign of Jayavarman VII, was equated with the city of the gods, while the asura demons, who had battled against the deva to try and capture that city, represented the Chams. Any Cham attempt to capture Angkor Thom would be, like that of the asuras, doomed to failure. These ideas are expressed in some of the magnificent reliefs carved in stone that decorate the walls of many of the monuments at Angkor. And their purpose was not merely decorative: at Angkor Wat depictions in bas-relief both of the gods and of Suryavarman's army in battle against the Cham enemy, or in victorious procession after defeating them, bestowed an additional talismanic power on the protective walls. These vibrant narrative scenes [76] are among the greatest artistic achievements of twelfth-century Angkor.

74 Causeway at Preah Khan, the site of Jayavarman VII's first capital at Angkor in the 12th century.

Another element of Khmer monuments that was believed to wield an important protective power was the lintel, and it was in carving lintels that the artistic skills of Khmer craftsmen reached their highest point. Both lintels and pediments contained talismanic force, and often bore depictions of deities and of tutelary monsters and demons. The finest lintels in Khmer art are almost certainly those produced in the ninth century during the reign of Indravarman. These are remarkable for the quality of both craftsmanship and composition, with a central deity flanked on each side by an elegantly curved naga covered with an agglomeration of figures and scrolling foliage, in a balanced but flamboyant style. Later examples in Angkor at East Mebon approach the stylistic elegance of these earlier lintels, with rich swirls of foliage to each side of the central figure.

The artistic achievements at Angkor are astounding, both in terms of architecture and sculpture. Among the most exquisite carvings are those at the temple of Banteay Srei [75], some twenty kilometres from Angkor Thom, consecrated towards the end of the tenth century. The delicate modelling of the many figures of heavenly devata, especially of their serene faces, makes them masterpieces of Khmer art. Of comparable quality are the narrative decorative panels on the pediments of the library façades, the graceful treatment of both the figures and their surroundings unsurpassed. The themes of these reliefs are derived from epics such as the Ramayana, which provides the subject matter for much of the art of both mainland Southeast Asia and the islands.

As on the mainland, maritime Southeast Asia is likely to have been linked with India through trade from the early centuries AD. The first tangible evidence of Hinduism is in seven sacrificial columns from the fourth century, found at Kutai in Borneo. But in the islands it is on Java that by far the most Hindu remains are found. The first substantial Hindu monuments are the Shivaite structures at the Dieng plateau, dating from the seventh century. Although there is a superficial resemblance between these single-chamber structures and some Indian temples, especially those of south India, the style does not follow any one prototype, and the decorative embellishments are clearly original. There is a pronounced entrance porch at the front leading to the central chamber where the principal image was probably housed, with false doors on the other sides, housing subsidiary statuary. Unusually on Java, while retaining the heads of a bull, goose and the man-eagle Garuda, the mounts of the principal gods at Dieng

75 The goddess Lakshmi (Sri) flanked by two elephants above an image of Garuda. Detail of carving on the interior pediment of the east porch of the east gopura of the second enclosure of Banteay Srei, Cambodia.

76 Relief showing a scene from the Mahabharata during the battle of Kurukshetra between the Pandavas and the Kurawas. Angkor Wat, western gallery, south wing.

are depicted with human bodies, and the god seated on their shoulders.

The most famous Hindu temple complex in Java is Candi Loro Jonggrang, at Prambanan, near Yogyakarta, with an inscription dating it to the mid-ninth century [77]. Again there are three main temples in a row, facing east. The principal temple, the middle of the three, is dedicated to Shiva, while those to Brahma and Vishnu are at either side of it. Opposite each of the three is a shrine, originally for the mount of each of the three gods. In only the central one does the statue remain: that of Nandi, the bull. Two smaller structures close to the north and south gates and eight tiny boundary candi are also contained within the surrounding wall, which separates this central area from the surrounding space, itself once studded with 224 small shrines, symmetrically arranged in four descending rows parallel to the four containing walls. Outside this courtyard is another, which must once have contained the buildings, made of more perishable materials, in which the activities involved in maintaining the temple and its devotees took place.

Of all the structures at Prambanan, the now restored Shiva temple is the tallest, rising steeply skywards, slender and graceful. The angles between the floors of the stepped roof are elided by clusters of miniature towers so that base, body and roof merge

77 The 9th-century Shiva temple at Candi Loro Jonggrang, Prambanan, Central Java, flanked by smaller temples dedicated to Brahma and Vishnu.

78 Stone sculpted images of celestial beings from the upper level of the balustrade above the terrace of the Shiva temple, Candi Loro Jonggrang, Prambanan, Central Java. Height 600 mm.

almost imperceptibly into one. Like the other two temples, the Shiva temple is built on an elevated terrace on which is an outer balustrade, forming a gallery around the base of the temple body. Around the lower body of the temple itself are twenty-four panels, some of which depict seated *lokapala*, or guardians of the cardinal points, flanked by attendants. On the inner side of the balustrade wall is the main part of a local version of the Ramayana story, which is continued in the Brahma temple. On the outer wall of the balustrade, flanked at intervals by other heavenly beings [78], are sixty-two groups of celestial dancers and musicians in whose figures both the elegance and ecstasy of the dance movements are conveyed.

The scenes from the Ramayana on the inner walls of the balustrade are animated, with the figures of the principal characters interacting in dynamic fashion. Servants and other minor figures also respond to what they are witnessing, as do the birds and animals frequently depicted in the surrounding areas of landscape or forest. The sculptures capture scenes of daily life with humour as well as energy [79], and there is a pervading sense of the power with which the Hindu gods imbue the world. The inspiration is Javanese, with local plants and animals, vernacular

79 Scenes from the Ramayana depicted in relief on the inside of the balustrade surrounding Candi Loro Jonggrang. *above* The monkey kings Sugriva and Valin fight, watched from the left by Rama. *below* Rama shoots an arrow at the ogress Talaka, watched by a creature depicted with characteristic realism. Heights 700 × 1950 mm; 770 × 2000 mm.

architecture and domestic detail informing the world portrayed. The style, too, differs from Indian art, with more gentle forms and less voluptuous female figures. Where there is sensuality it is subtle, and erotic scenes of deities locked in embrace with their shaktis, their female counterparts, are absent.

The statuary of Central Java is characterized by its full, rounded forms. Bodies are full-fleshed, solid and strong, often with a gentle sway and the weight resting to one side. Sculptural figures in Javanese temples tend to belong to one of two groups. The first is formed by the three gods of the Trimurti: Brahma, Vishnu and Shiva. The second group, associated with Shiva temples, consists of Durga, Ganesha [81], and sometimes the sage Agastya, with the two guardians Mahakala and Nandisvara often

80 The elegant tower of Candi Jawi in East Java is some 17 metres high. It was erected in the 13th century to commemorate the death of Kretanagara, the last king of Singasari, whose espousal of both Hinduism and Buddhism is reflected in the form of the candi.

flanking the entrance to Shiva's chamber. Shiva himself is occasionally represented by a lingam, but when he is shown in bodily form he is usually identified, as are other deities, by attributes derived from Indian art. Nonetheless, the sculpture of the Central Javanese period includes features that give it its own distinctive character. Images of Ganesha, for example, tend to show him seated with the soles of his feet together, a form that is unusual in India. Both Ganesha and Agastya appear frequently in Central Java, the latter far more so than in India or elsewhere in Southeast Asia.

In the early part of the tenth century the centre of Javanese power shifted from Central to East Java. This was followed by a long hiatus in the construction of religious monuments and the carving of associated stone sculptures. A few structures survive, mostly royal funerary temples. These candi are more slender and less symmetrical in plan than those of Central Java. The main towers of East Javanese temples, instead of being at the centre of the complex and surrounded by concentric enclosures, were placed at the back of the compound, and the courtyards set one behind the other [80]. Candi Jawi, founded to commemorate King Kretanagara, who died in 1292, is dedicated to Shiva-Buddha, a Hindu temple with a stupa at its apex. This combination of Hindu and Buddhist elements in one monument typifies the way the two religious traditions co-existed for many centuries in Indonesia.

Kretanagara participated in another feature of Javanese religion of the time, Tantrism, in which the devotee could acquire supernatural powers through various means. Tantric elements sometimes appeared in both Hindu and Buddhist practice. They included the use of hand gestures, magic (including the use of mantras, magical utterances), and the worship of shaktis. Gurus taught the secret death rituals or sexual practices described in Tantric texts, rituals that led to states of heightened consciousness. Tantric practices are indicated in iconographical form in the depiction of Bhairava, an aspect of Shiva sometimes called Mahakala, who often appears with a necklace of snakes and a garland of skulls.

East Javanese statuary in which deceased kings and queens were presented as deified beings departed less obviously from previous forms. However, in this period there is a stronger sense of portraiture, and the positions of her hands frequently differ from those in classical Indian statuary of deities. In the Singasari period, lotus stems growing from the base may appear to either side of the figure [83]. Overall, the figures in East Javanese statuary

81 Stone sculpture of Ganesha, Central Java. 9th–10th century. Height 800 mm.

are more slender than those of Central Java, and there is often a greater sense of symmetry. Jewelry and other adornments tend to be more prominent. After the start of Majapahit rule in 1293, the main focus in East Javanese art seems to have shifted from statuary to the production of ritual paraphernalia: ceremonial finials, elaborate lamps and especially bells, all in bronze, together with extremely fine jewelry and regalia in gold [82]. All this metalwork is characterized by a refined elegance and complexity of detail, worked by highly skilled artisans.

Permeating the art of this period is the presence of a multitude of beings drawn from Hindu narrative traditions, which included such tales as the Arjuna Wiwaha, the Ramayana, the story of Sri Tanjung and the Tantri tales. This narrative thrust is also present in the reliefs with which temples were embellished. As with the architecture, the style of the narrative reliefs from the East Javanese period also differs from that of Central Java. Two opposing styles are identified as having developed during this period. One was more romantic in mood, with natural landscapes in which human figures are depicted in soft, gently modelled forms. The other, now generally referred to as 'wayang style' [84] presents figures both human and supernatural in two-dimensional form, as in the wayang shadow theatre, against increasingly stylized landscapes that came to appear magical, supernatural. Some reliefs combined both styles, however.

82 Repoussé gold plaque depicting a scene from the Ramayana in which monkey warriors, building a causeway to help rescue Rama's wife Sita from Lanka, are startled by a crab. Kediri, East Java. 14th–15th century.

83 Four-armed image of Shiva on a double lotus pedestal, thought by some to be a portrait of the deceased Singasari king Anushpati as Shiva, possibly from Candi Kidal, East Java. Late 13th century. Height 1230 mm.

At the beginning of the sixteenth century, the Hindu court of Majapahit was forced, under pressure from the Islamic state of Demak, to abandon Java. The royal family and many members of the aristocracy took refuge in Bali, taking much of their artistic heritage, including artists, with them. Surviving Balinese temples from before that time had often been built into rock faces, perhaps because such places were thought to be the dwelling places of deities, perhaps for protection from earthquakes. Most of these places of worship did not contain inner spaces for housing the image of the deity. One exception was Goa Gajah, the Elephant Cave, a temple probably dating from the second half of the eleventh century [85]. Female figures at the bathing place beside it, which function as water spouts, are reminiscent of those at Belahan in East Java. The scroll motifs and the images of rocks at the front of the cave also resemble designs from Javanese architecture of the period.

The persistence of the Hindu tradition in Bali means that construction and renovation of temples and associated statuary continues. Much of the iconography follows the models set down in previous centuries. Thus the structure of the split gate, which appears in a temple at Trowulan in East Java, can be seen widely in

84 Scene from the Mahabharata depicted in *wayang*-style reliefs at Candi Jago, East Java. 13th century.

Bali, especially in the southern part of the island. Other structures depicted in reliefs of the East Javanese period also appear in Bali, and suggestions that Balinese art represents a continuation of the art of East Java are not entirely unfounded. For example, *kala* heads over many Balinese temple entrances are, as in East Java, particularly fierce, with bulging eyes, thick eyebrows and prominent fangs. Nevertheless, Balinese culture was never completely overrun by that of Java, and retained its own vitality and distinctiveness, which have survived into the twenty-first century.

The narrative tradition, so evident in Java, also pervades Balinese art [86]. A similar set of story cycles is told, containing lessons about morality and spirituality as well as exploring ideas of kingship and release from worldly cares. Balinese legends also provide subject matter, the characters portrayed in a wide range of media, from temple hangings, embroideries and other textiles [87] to shadow puppets, stone reliefs and paintings on glass. It is the characters and stories of the Hindu epics, however, that represent the most powerful unifying force in Southeast Asian art. The stories travelled throughout the region, partly through interaction between the courts. Performances staged for visiting

85 Goa Gajah, a cave hermitage in Bali probably dating back to the 11th century. The demon mouth carved into the rock probably represents Kala, the god of time, a manifestation of Shiva in his destructive aspect.

foreign dignitaries were one means of the exchange of ideas, but considerable influence probably resulted from the transfer of art and artists themselves.

In maritime Southeast Asia the Mahabharata became the most popular of the Indian epics, providing the basis for most of the wayang kulit shows performed in association with court and village rituals. The story centres on the five Pandawa brothers and their Korawa cousins, as they struggle for control of the disputed kingdom of Hastina. Two of the Pandawa brothers who particularly stand out are the mighty Bima, recognizable by his size and his lengthy thumbnail, and the noble Arjuna [89]. Krishna, who

acts as an adviser to the Pandawas, is an incarnation of the god Vishnu, and it is he who encourages Arjuna to fight in battle against his cousins in order to restore justice. The battle is not simply one of good against evil; characters on both sides have strengths and weaknesses that provide lessons about duty, self-discipline and honour much discussed by audiences. In both Bali and Java, local figures were introduced; these act in some ways as intermediaries between the drama and the audience. Characters from the Mahabharata also appear in sculpture from the Majapahit period. Striking sculptures of Bima and figures from the Garudeya, a Javanese poem which combines Indian legend with local elements, were found at Candi Sukuh in Central Java, constructed in the first half of the fifteenth century and dedicated to Bima himself.

On the mainland it was the Ramayana that had the most long-lasting impact on artistic representation. Prince Rama's search for Sita, abducted by the evil Ravana, is the basis of most plots in dance performances as well as in the shadow theatre [88]. Among the other key characters are Rama's brother, Laksman, and Hanuman, the white monkey who leads the forces of the monkey

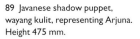

89 Javanese shadow puppet, wayang kulit, representing Arjuna. Height 475 mm.

army across the causeway he has built to Ravana's island home of Lanka. This tale is depicted on murals surrounding both the Royal Palace at Bangkok and the Silver Pagoda in Phnom Penh [90]. Thai kings have been associated with Rama since the founding of the Chakri dynasty in 1782, when General Chakri took the title of Rama I. Succeeding kings have continued the connection. The Ramayana is widely interpreted in Buddhist Thailand as a 'Jataka' story, one recounting an earlier incarnation of the Buddha as Prince Rama.

As well as these figures, other elements of Hindu art persist in contemporary mainland Southeast Asia. Hindu deities appear outside Buddhist shrines, where they are regarded as the protectors of Buddhism. Images of supernatural beings common to both Hindu and Buddhist worlds are found decorating lacquer cabinets containing Buddhist scriptures and mother of pearl trays for Buddhist offerings. Characteristics more central to the Buddhist art of the region are the theme of the next chapter.

90 Hanuman enlarges his body and places Phra Ram's pavilion in his mouth. Mural depicting a scene from the Ramayana in the galleries of the Temple of the Emerald Buddha, Bangkok. 19th century.

Chapter 4   The imprint of the Buddha

The teachings of the Buddha have had an influence on the art of
Southeast Asia that is thought to date back to the third century
BC. Shakyamuni, otherwise Siddharta Gautama, the founder of
what was to become one of the world's great religions, was born
around the sixth century BC in the Terai mountains of Nepal, the
son of a local ruler. In his spiritual and religious quest he turned his
back on riches and power, and the story of his life and his lives in
earlier incarnations inspired much of the art of those who
followed his teachings. The Buddha, the 'Enlightened One',
accepted many of the tenets of Hinduism, and much Hindu
iconography is retained within Buddhism. At the core of his
teachings, however, was the search for release from suffering, and
his discourses set down guidelines for the individual to take
responsibility for his own actions rather than looking to the gods
to intervene.

By the time Buddhism arrived in Southeast Asia, differences
of opinion among members of the monkhood had resulted in a
split within the discipline. Early teachings had emphasized the
need for each individual to strive to attain enlightenment, and
thus release from the cycle of rebirth. The Mahayana school,
which had begun to develop a hundred years after the death of
the Buddha, considered this to be unrealistic, and emphasized
rather the body of bodhisattvas, those who had postponed their
own chance for nirvana in order to help others. Such saints
became for many the main focus of the religion. In addition,
Mahayanism embraced a belief in five great Buddhas, four of
whom guarded the cardinal directions, while another, Vairocana,
stood at the centre. Each of these is associated with a number of
other deities and bodhisattvas. The most important of them,
Avalokiteshvara, is associated with the Buddha Amithaba in the
west. While the art of Theravada Buddhism, the old tradition,
produced chiefly images of the historical Buddha Shakyamuni

91 An image of the Buddha in
bhumisparsa mudra, the most
commonly depicted in Southeast
Asian art. Borobudur, Central Java.
9th century.

92 Four-armed bronze Sriwijayan Avalokiteshvara discovered in what is now southern Thailand. 8th to 9th century. Height 340 mm.

himself, and of scenes from his life and former lives from which lessons might be drawn, the art of Mahayana Buddhism included a great many images of other Buddhas and bodhisattvas through whom devotees sought salvation. In Southeast Asia, ideas from both traditions are embodied in monuments, manuscripts, religious statuary and votive tablets, as well as in the paraphernalia of religious practice.

According to tradition it was King Asoka, ruler of a central Indian kingdom, who spread Buddhism to Southeast Asia. It was under his auspices that the third Buddhist Council was held at Patna in India in 250 BC, after which he sent out nine missionaries to other countries. One was 'The Land of Gold', widely believed to have been Burma. Buddhism was probably introduced to the region by such missionaries and other wandering scholars who travelled across the region in the centuries that followed. Some would have journeyed from India by the Silk Road to northern China; others by sea through the Straits of Malacca to the coast of present-day Vietnam and on to southern China. A number of these monks left accounts of their journeys, which show that they were often forced by the seasonal winds to stop for several months at a time at places along the route. Here they might study the holy scriptures or disseminate to others the teachings embodied in the sacred texts. Some probably settled permanently. Many carried with them models of stupas, shrines containing holy relics, or figures of the Buddha in metal or stone, and these were copied by locals who took up the religion.

In maritime Southeast Asia, the first great kingdom to espouse Buddhism was that of Sriwijaya, whose base moved between centres on the banks of the Musi and Batanghari rivers in southeastern Sumatra. It was closely linked with neighbouring Malaya, but its political influence also extended at one time over parts of Java, the Malay Peninsula and into southern Thailand. Sriwijaya's period of dominance in the region lasted from the eighth to the thirteenth centuries AD. Although relatively few remains of its architecture have been discovered, many sculpted images have survived, among them a number of bronze statues of the bodhisattva Avalokiteshvara, the embodiment of compassion [92]. These smoothly finished figures are slender and upright, with the upper limbs in graceful postures. Some of the Sriwijayan kings established foundations at the Mahayana university of Nalanda in northeastern India, where immigrant communities flourished. Not surprisingly, there is considerable evidence of Indian influence in Sriwijayan sculpture, seen for example in the draping of the robes.

Buddhism left a much stronger imprint in Java, where it was introduced by the Sriwijayan Sailendra dynasty early in the ninth century. The Buddhist monuments from this period existed alongside a flourishing Shivaite tradition, and many contain images of Hindu deities such as Kubera, the god of wealth and guardian of the north. By this time, artists and craftsmen were no longer merely imitating Indian forms, but were developing a genuine Javanese style. This culminated in the best-known and undoubtedly most significant Buddhist structure in Java, Borobudur [93]. The Buddhist monuments of Java often reflected the structure of the cosmos, as did Hindu religious architecture. Constructed over the peak of a natural hill, Borobudur appears like a stone mountain, its stepped platforms crowned with a bell-shaped stupa. The word 'stupa' originally referred to the mound that covered a relic or ashes of the Buddha, but later came to denote the monument built above relics of a religious person. It is not clear whether Borobudur served such a function. It is not a temple, since it does not house an image of a god to be worshipped or appeased by the donation of offerings. Borobudur does, however, represent the Buddha and his teachings, and was clearly intended to be experienced by circumambulation. Walking around the base and then the eight terraces, with the right side of

93 Aerial view of Borobudur, Central Java. 9th century.

the body facing inwards towards the sacred building, the devotee follows a series of reliefs setting out the Buddhist conception of the journey towards enlightenment. The higher one climbs, the further one is removed from scenes of the everyday world of desire, passing from depictions of the lives of the Buddha in the world of form to the upper sphere of formlessness.

The five lower terraces of the monument are built on a square plan, a shape representing the earth, while the three higher terraces are circular, symbolic of the sky or the heavens. Carved into the walls at the base of the monument are scenes of human life, depicting good and bad deeds, together with the corresponding rewards and punishments. These scenes are shielded from view by stones which skirt the monument at the lowest level, though why this should be so has never been definitively answered. On the lower terraces there are balustrades surrounding the walkway, into which are set niches housing images of Buddhas. The visitor sees reliefs to his left and right: the outer ones depict Jataka stories, episodes from the previous lives of the Buddha; on the inner walls the reliefs progress from incidents in the life of the historical Buddha [94] on the first terrace, gradually rising through episodes from the adventures of the Bodhisattva Sudhana in his search for enlightenment. The final stages of these panels at the top level

94 Relief from the upper panel of the inner wall of the first gallery of Borobudur, depicting Prince Siddhartha cutting off his hair as a sign of his renunciation of the material world. 9th century.

show Buddha figures enthroned in the heavens together with other celestial beings. On the three circular terraces at the top are seventy-two images of the Buddha in a posture of teaching, each enclosed in a bell-shaped cover, sometimes referred to as a stupa, that is punctured to resemble latticework. At the centre of the uppermost terrace is the central stupa, inside which is an empty cell. This may once have contained a figure or relic of the Buddha, or it may always have been empty.

The Buddha images at Borobudur clearly owe much to their Indian forbears, but there is a difference. They are sculpted in a softer, more naturalistic style, with gentle, subtle contours that speak of a calm, divine beauty [91]. The carving of the reliefs echoes this grace, and again the modelling of the figures is more restrained than in Indian sculpture. The emphasis, especially in the scenes of heavenly beings and those of the life of the Buddha, is on balance and symmetry, with a soft and harmonious sense of movement. There is none of the drama, vigour and energy that characterize the Hindu reliefs at Loro Jonggrang, where the power with which the gods imbue the natural world is felt at every turn. The carving in the narrow galleries of the lower terraces at Borobudur is, however, quite dense and full, so that on reaching the open circular terraces there is a sense of space which comes as a release and lifts the spirit upwards.

The achievement of Borobudur is in the totality of its form. This vast monument is a harmonious composition expressing both the shape of the cosmos and man's spiritual quest, which is re-enacted in the journey through which the structure and its reliefs are experienced. The association of the lower parts with profanity, and the climb towards simpler and more serene forms, is analogous to the progression to which Buddhist teaching encourages humans to aspire – away from the material world towards the world of formlessness, and eventual salvation and unification with the ultimate reality through the annihilation of self.

The large Buddhist complexes of Candi Plaosan and Candi Sewu, also in Central Java, both date from the same century as Borobudur. At Candi Plaosan the ideas of Mahayana Buddhism are revealed both in inscriptions and in the sculptures. A large number of statues of Buddhas and bodhisattvas [95] were housed there, which inscriptions show were intended to reflect the radiance of the sun and moon both symbolically and actually. The surfaces of the statues are softly carved so that the light reveals smooth, calm gradations of tone, resulting in a mood of tranquillity and order. At the centre are two tall buildings, one sponsored by the king and the other by the queen, while the outer buildings were erected through contributions from lesser dignitaries. The complex thus reflects in its structure the order of both the kingdom and the cosmos.

For the next three hundred years no new Buddhist monuments were constructed by the Javanese kings, whose monuments were for the most part dedicated to Shiva and the Hindu deities associated with him. It was not until the thirteenth century, when the centre of power had moved to East Java, that Buddhism once again received royal patronage. The last ruler of the kingdom of Singasari, King Kertanagara, seems to have embraced both Buddhism and Shivaism. In Java the practice of both had at this time absorbed many elements of Tantrism, in which various rituals were employed in a belief that they would ease the path to enlightenment and nirvana. Mystery surrounds the precise nature of the acts involved, but the link between cosmic and sexual energy, and the correspondences made between sexual and spiritual ecstasy, suggest that sexual union was an integral part of the search for release from worldly existence. Some sculptures include depictions of skulls, possibly indicating the practice of human sacrifice. A magnificent fourteenth-century statue of the Sumatran King Adityawarman as Bhairava shows him standing on a corpse surrounded by skulls, his skirt cloth covered

95 Stone sculpture of the Bodhisattva Samantabhadra, Candi Plaosan, Central Java. 8th to 9th century.

with repeating patterns of skull images [96]. In the headdress is a small bodhisattva image, revealing the Buddhist connections of this version of the Bhairava cult. Similar Bhairava statues from Java contrast markedly with the serene sculptures of the earlier, Central Javanese period. The emphasis in these works is on vigour, strength and power, reflected in the forceful carving and strong open features of the faces.

Buddhist remains from the period after Singasari's prominence are few in maritime Southeast Asia. It was on the mainland that Buddhism continued to thrive, and to inform the work of artists right up to the present day. Here the origins of Buddhism also lie earlier than in the islands, dating back to the kingdom of the Pyu in present-day Burma, described in Chinese texts of the second century AD. There were several centres of Pyu culture, the most important in Sri Kshetra, near Prome; in Beikthano, between Sri Kshetra and Mandalay; and in Halin in the north. The first true arch in Southeast Asia is found in the architecture of early Prome, and though arches were also built at Pagan they are not found

96 Statue of Adityawarman as Bhairava, found at Padang Lawas, Sumatra. 14th century. Height 4410 mm.

elsewhere; in other parts of the region builders relied on
corbelling to create spaces within their monuments. Outside the
walls and guarding the entrances to Sri Kshetra were three huge
pagodas of a distinctive elongated barrel shape, built on a circular
platform. Although a number of small brick-built temples remain
in the city, only the three great stupas can be confidently ascribed
to the Pyu period.

Much more evidence remains of the sculpture of the Pyu,
especially Buddha images from Sri Kshetra. Monumental stones,
some carved in low relief, and some grouped together, probably
represent the continuation of a pre-Buddhist megalithic tradition.
As well as stone stelae, there are votive stupas, terracotta
sculptural plaques, stone and gilt-bronze Buddha images, and gilt-
bronze bodhisattvas. The styles of these sculptures vary, and
suggest influences from southern India, from the Gupta culture of
fourth- and fifth-century northern India and later eastern Indian
Mahayanistic ideas. Votive stupas are sometimes four-sided,
reflecting the four Buddhas of the Mahayana tradition, each facing

97 Clay votive tablet from Pagan,
with the Buddha in *bhumisparsa
mudra*, flanked by two of his
disciples, Mogallana and Sariputta.
Burma, 11th to 12th century.

a cardinal direction. Some later works contain echoes of the style and iconography of works from Indonesia and peninsular Thailand, showing that by the eighth century the Pyu had become part of a more international artistic world.

At Angkor, although there is earlier evidence of Buddhism, it was during the reign of King Jayavarman VII (1181–1218) that it received the greatest patronage. The most important figure was Avalokiteshvara, who was depicted in a variety of manifestations, including that of Prajnaparamita, the goddess of wisdom. Visible representations of the Buddha at Angkor convey a sense of serenity and benevolence, perhaps representing the king himself and how he preferred to be seen. The faces at the gateways to the city of Angkor Thom and in the towers of Jayavarman VII's state temple, Bayon, have been interpreted in various ways, as portraits of the king as Avalokiteshvara, or sometimes simply as guardians of the cardinal points [98]. Characteristic of these haunting faces is a benign smile on gently curving lips. Statues of the Buddha from this period often show him seated on three coils of the naga

98 Face carved in stone over the southern gateway to Angkor Thom, Cambodia.

99 The Buddha in *dhyana mudra*, the posture of meditation, raised on the coils of the naga Mucilinda and sheltered by his hood. This is the central image of the Bayon looking from the east; some say it depicts Jayavarman VII. Angkor, Cambodia.

100 Standing crowned Buddha in *abhaya mudra*, the posture of dispelling fear. On the palms of the hands is the Wheel of the Law. Khmer, Angkor Wat style, 12th century. Height 425 mm.

Mucilinda and sheltered by its hood [99]. Another image prevalent in the second half of the twelfth century shows the Buddha crowned and decorated, perhaps as the ruler of heaven, perhaps a reference to the supreme Buddha of Tantric Buddhism, the adi-Buddha [100]. The crown typically consists of a central band flaring outward as it rises, decorated with regular rows of geometric patterns such as roundels and beads, with lotus buds edging the upper rim. Large pendant earrings and a necklace of rows of jewels echo the style of the crown. The eyes are downcast, with fine eyebrows meeting over the nose; the lips are full and fleshy, the face square with a curved band above the hairline.

Although these styles spread to other areas under Khmer rule such as Lopburi in central Thailand, it was not Mahayana but

Theravada Buddhism that later became the dominant faith in Thailand. There is some evidence of Theravada Buddhism in the art of the Pyu, but the people who were largely responsible for its earliest dissemination were the Mon, and in particular those living in the kingdom known as Dvaravati, in what is now central Thailand. The term Dvaravati has been applied to the art of many Mon kingdoms in this area. While Dvaravati art shows evidence of Sri Lankan, Gupta and later Sriwijayan influence, Dvaravati artists developed a distinctive style of their own. They worked in bronze, stucco and terracotta as well as in limestone, but the stone available was not easy to work and affected the style of the carving. Figures tend to be solid and heavy, and for standing poses the drape of the long robes may have been determined by the need to support the rest of the sculpture. Even so, Dvaravati sculptors included in their repertoire a great range of postures and styles of drapery [101]. The faces of the Buddha images are characterized by a broad, rounded shape with downward-sloping,

101 Dvaravati stone sculpture of the Buddha in *dhyana mudra*, meditating under the Bodhi tree. Found at Dong Si Mahaphot, Thailand. Height 1030 mm

102 View of Pagan. To the left the slender tower of the Ananda temple, built at the start of the twelfth century, rises from the plain. In the centre is the That-byin-nyu, thought to have been built towards the end of the reign of Sithu I in the second half of the century.

103 The Shwezigon was completed by King Kyanzittha, who came to power in 1084. Later additions and restoration work have earned merit for a variety of subsequent benefactors. Pagan, Burma.

downcast eyes above which arched eyebrows stretch in a
continuous line. The curls of the hair are large and flat, curving
anticlockwise toward the centre (as they always do in depictions
of the Buddha). Standing Buddhas often show both arms in the
same gesture, usually that of teaching.

Dvaravati came under Khmer control in the eleventh century
and was later incorporated into the Thai kingdoms that followed,
but nonetheless the form of Theravada Buddhism espoused by the
Mon was adopted and subsumed into the cultures of these more
powerful states. In Burma too, Theravada Buddhism had become
the dominant mode of religion by the eleventh century, as a result,
at least in part, of Mon influence. By this time, Sri Lanka was
regarded as the source of the purest form of the religion, and
missions were sent between Burma and Sri Lanka resulting in an
increasingly close relationship between the two Buddhist
establishments. It became a frequent practice for monks to be
sent to Sri Lanka so that they could be ordained there into the
Mahavira order, which had first set down the Pali canon. Sri
Lankan monks travelling to Burma took with them sacred
scriptures and holy relics, and it was to Sri Lanka that Southeast
Asian rulers later looked for models on which to base their
religious monuments.

One way that Burmese rulers legitimized and consolidated
their power was by endowing religious monuments. The
construction of monuments, installation of Buddha images and
embellishment of religious buildings with didactic murals were all
ways of earning merit, which could help the donor in his
aspirations to be reborn in heaven. In the late eleventh century
King Kyanzittha endowed many foundations as well as contributing
towards repairs to the shrine at Bodgaya where the historical
Buddha had achieved enlightenment. He also completed the
Shwezigon in Pagan [103]. The Shwezigon is a pagoda, a monument
containing a relic chamber, and is composed of an octagonal 'band'
built on three terraces supporting a bell-shaped stupa, a form
inspired by Sri Lankan architecture. On the upper terrace there is
a smaller version of the main stupa at each corner, and at the
middle of each terrace, facing the cardinal points, is a stairway.
Facing each stairway is a chamber containing a standing Buddha
image in *vitarka mudra*, the posture of elucidation. The Shwezigon
became a model for later stupas.

Kyanzittha also sponsored the Ananda temple, a place for
meditation, which derives its form not from Indian models but
from earlier indigenous architecture in the region [102]. Compared

104 Marble Buddha image in *bhumisparsa mudra*, Burma, 17th century or earlier. Height 876.3 mm.

105 Buddha image in *bhumisparsa mudra*, in gilded wood. Burmese Buddha images are especially hard to date; this one is probably Shan, and may date from the 18th century. 605 × 330 × 235 mm.

with Shwezigon, the impression is one of lightness and elevation, with the spire supported by a more slender tower, and the mass of the lower levels disguised behind a base wall decorated with ornate arched gateways and mouldings of stupas. The horizontal axis is lifted by the corner stupas on the lower two terraces and the small spires on the higher terrace, which echo the temple's crowning feature. The lower terraces are decorated with glazed plaques showing scenes from the Jataka tales.

Burma became the centre from which Theravada Buddhist orthodoxy was disseminated to the rest of the region, and it had a part to play in the spread of artistic concepts and styles, including those derived from Sri Lankan tradition. Influence was spread partly through Buddha images, which appear in a number of forms, including votive tablets [97] and free-standing sculptures [104, 105]. After the removal of the Burmese capital to Ava in the seventeenth century, Buddha images were increasingly made of marble and bronze, and this together with influence from the powerful Thai kingdom of Ayutthaya may be the reason for the smoother finish of the styles dating from this period. Flame-like protuberances above the *usnisa*, the Buddha's cranial protuberance, were a common feature of this period, as were crowned Buddhas, a reference not only to the high status of the Buddha but also to his humbling of King Jambupati. After the conquest of Ayutthaya in 1767 and the removal of the Burmese capital to Mandalay in 1857, images of the Buddha took on a more lifelike appearance, with particular attention given to the draping of the robes, which in standing figures were often spread by his raised arms.

The Burmese, Khmer and Mon ruled various parts of the area we now know as Thailand until the thirteenth century, when a new power began to emerge. Tai-speaking groups who had made their way southward began to establish themselves as a major force in parts of the region. The first great Thai kingdom, Lan Na, was established at Chieng Mai in the north in the late thirteenth century. In subsequent centuries, the kingdoms of Sukhothai, Ayutthaya and eventually Ratanakosin, or Bangkok, came to dominate. The art of these and other lesser Thai courts was at first strongly influenced by that of their predecessors, the Mons, as was their religion, but the art with which they expressed their new-found beliefs gradually developed a style of its own. The main components of the Thai monastery, or *wat*, can be seen in the complexes in the earliest of these cities. The various buildings are

106 Clusters of chedi surround the *ubosot* at Wat Konkharam, Potcharam, Ratchaburi, Thailand.

arranged within an enclosing wall, the most important being the *ubosot*, the assembly hall where new monks are initiated. The sacred nature of this building is indicated by eight marker stones, or *sema*, usually in the shape of a lotus petal, which surround it. To the west of this building, and constructed in a similar style, is the *viharn*, the main meeting hall which houses the principal Buddha image and which may be entered by members of the lay community.

Sometimes a monastic complex also contains a library for storing sacred texts and sometimes there is a bell tower. Most also include *prangs* or *chedis*, structures containing holy relics [106]. The prang is common in complexes influenced by Khmer forms, themselves owing much to those of India. It is a symbol of potency, suggestive of a closed lotus bud but also reminiscent of the lingam. Some prangs are mounted above the roofs of royal buildings, others may be on a tiered plinth. The prang itself consists of seven

107 Bronze Sukhothai Buddha image in *bhumisparsa mudra*. 14th century

tiers, a reference to the layers of heaven [109]. The Thai chedi, or stupa, is normally set on a platform of three levels representing the Traiphum, or three worlds. Above it is a *mongkut* or spire made up of thirty-three disks, which refer to the thirty-three Buddhist heavens, inhabited by beings at various stages in the journey to release.

Of the various kingdoms that have dominated what is now Thailand, it was Sukhothai, based in north-central Thailand from the mid-thirteenth century until it faded at the end of the fourteenth, that set the standard for the art of the Thai region in all the centuries that followed; later periods have consistently referred back to it as the golden age of Thai art. The style of bronze Buddha images created by Sukhothai artists is quite distinct from what went before, and those that followed rarely matched its ethereal beauty. All four postures referred to in the ancient texts were reproduced in Sukhothai statuary: seated, standing, reclining and walking [107]. Depictions of the Buddha

108 Bronze Sukhothai image of the walking Buddha in *vitarka mudra*, the posture of elucidation, in which the first finger and thumb of the raised hand form a circle. 14th century. Height 2200 mm.

walking are extremely rare elsewhere [108]. The aim of the monks who modelled the Buddha's figure was not, however, to innovate. They were striving to follow as closely as possible the descriptions set down in early religious texts, some Sanskrit and some Pali. Most of these were poetic in their style, and gave indications of how a Buddha-to-be might be recognized. But Sukhothai sculptors attempted to replicate quite literally references to the the thirty-two major and eighty minor marks of a great man. These included Buddha's arms being 'like an elephant's trunk' and his fingers curved back like the petals of a lotus flower about to bloom. Finishes of bronze and gilt allowed the sculptors to suggest the smooth skin to which dust would not adhere, as well as the radiance emanating from the Buddha as he achieved enlightenment.

In contrast to the distinctiveness of Sukhothai sculpture, architecture was indebted to a range of precursors, Khmer, Mon and Sri Lankan. Only from the mid-fourteenth century did Thai architecture develop a more distinctive style, when another Thai kingdom, Ayutthaya, grew strong enough to challenge Sukhothai. Located in the far south around the rich Chao Phraya valley, it was

109 Khmer-style prang at the centre of Wat Ratchaburana, Ayutthaya. 15th century.

110 A scene from the *Culla-setthi-jataka*, the fourth of the Jataka tales, in which a young man acts on a remark overheard from the bodhisattva and becomes rich as a result. Mural on the east wall of the ambulatory, Ananda temple, Pagan, Burma. Late 18th century.

the kingdom of Ayutthaya that came to be known as Siam. In the first century-and-a-half of its existence, Ayutthayan rulers built more than two hundred wats. Many of the earliest were based on Khmer designs, with a central prang surrounded by courtyards and smaller prangs in a walled enclosure. These brick-built complexes were later covered in stucco and whitewashed, and topped with tiers of tiled roofs. There were few windows, and those that were included were usually only narrow slits. The chedi initially echoed the bell shape of the Sri Lankan stupa, but gradually the slopes of the shoulders were squared off and the spires became more slender. The prang of later Ayutthaya were also slimmer than their predecessors, giving a new lightness and elegance to Thai architecture.

In sculpture Ayutthaya's artist-monks were largely content to follow their forbears in the shaping of the Buddha's likeness, though there were some innovations. The principal medium was bronze, though images were also produced in stone. A central feature of Ayutthayan sculpture was the large size of the images, with many stone statues made in sections and others constructed in brick and covered in stucco. The popularity of standing Buddhas continued, though most Buddhas were still depicted in a seated position. The *dhyana mudra*, or meditating gesture, was more popular than it had been, and there was also more variety in the poses of the standing Buddhas. In his walking guise, the Buddha's weight shifted to his right side, and there was a corresponding change in the postion of the hands, with the left hand in *abhaya mudra*, the gesture of reassurance, rather than the right. As time went by, there was an increasing tendency to adorn the Buddha with jewelry, embroidery and ever more elaborate headdresses.

Wood carving also became particularly elaborate during the Ayutthayan period, especially on and around doorways, windows and ceilings. Murals were probably a widespread feature of Ayutthayan wats, though most of those remaining date from after the sack of Ayutthaya by the Burmese in 1767. Burmese murals, on the other hand, survive from a much earlier period. The best known of these are the murals from the Pagan period, presenting a rich miscellany of religious subjects including Mahayana and Tantric elements as well as Hindu deities and Jataka tales [110]. As the years went by, the range of material narrowed, so that by the seventeenth and eighteenth centuries nearly all depicted the life of the Buddha, or the tales of his previous incarnations. The latter were usually depicted beneath the life of the Buddha, with

III Footprints of the Buddha are objects of veneration in Buddhism and are often depicted in murals, manuscripts and sculptures. Sites of such footprints have become the destination for many pilgrims. Mural at Wat Na Phrathat, Pak Thong Chai, northeastern Thailand. Early 19th century.

the earliest at the bottom of the wall and the more enlightened further up in the hierarchy of images.

In the late eighteenth and nineteenth centuries there was a shift towards adopting an aerial perspective, and events no longer followed a linear progression, perhaps as a result of influence from Thai murals [III]. As with Burmese wall painting, the layout of murals in Thai temples generally follows a consistent pattern. Each wall of the assembly hall depicts a specific subject. Behind the main Buddha image, and so facing the devotee as he pays homage, are

scenes from the Traiphum. At the base of the wall are scenes from the lower hells, while at the top are the highest levels of existence. At the top of the south- and north-facing walls, to either side of the devotee, members of a divine congregation are depicted: *devata* (celestial beings) and *yaksha* (benign demons) which also turn to face the Buddha image; below them there may be scenes from the life of the Buddha. Opposite the main Buddha image, the back wall usually shows the Enlightenment of the Buddha in which he calls the earth to witness his victory over the demon Mara, while Thoranee, the Thai earth goddess, wrings out her hair to drown the demons.

While there are fragments of mural painting in Ayutthaya that survived the Burmese destruction of the city in 1767, there are more remnants of the Ayutthaya period in provincial temples outside the capital. Examples often show horizontal rows of devotees separated by bands of floral and vegetal decoration. Although they produce a repeating pattern of shapes, variations in the costume or posture of the figures prevent monotony, and both demons and devotees are depicted as individuals. Scenes within these murals tend to be surrounded by cascades of blossom or floral designs, a recurring element in Thai murals that is especially characteristic of this period. Murals also survive from Luang Prabang (now in Laos) and the northern kingdom of Lanna, where the style was often less formal. Those at the Phra Singh temple in Chiang Mai, for example, contain scenes of local village life in the lower registers of the north and south walls.

In the late eighteenth century the capital was moved to Bangkok. The kings of the new Chakri dynasty used art and ritual to establish continuity with the old kingdom and underline the legitimacy of their rule. Although few murals remained from Ayutthaya to act as models, surviving manuscripts may have

112 Illustration from an illuminated historical *parabaik*, showing the assassination of Prince Myingun, the brother of King Mindun, in 1866. Konbaung period, Burma. Each fold measures 70 × 410 mm.

113 Burmese court *parabaik* depicting the cosmic pillar rising from Mount Meru, which is surrounded by a gigantic fish. Late 19th century

provided inspiration for much of the Thai painting that followed. The three worlds of Buddhist cosmology were frequently depicted, as were other religious themes. The first building to be established in the complex at the Royal Palace in Bangkok was Wat Phra Keo, the temple housing the Emerald Buddha. The walls of the surrounding courtyard were decorated with paintings of scenes from the Ramakien, the Thai version of the Ramayana. Although the work has been renewed many times since, it remains typical of the early Bangkok period, and is echoed in the early twentieth-century paintings on the walls of the Cambodian royal palace courtyard. The style is conventional, with scenes shown from an aerial perspective. Figures tend to be two-dimensional and faces show little emotion. Mood is expressed by stylized gestures. Episodes are usually separated by elements of landscape such as trees, streams or walls, or sometimes a geometric zigzag. The Bangkok period was characterized by a lavish use of gold and a wider and more intense palette of colours than in the past. Backgrounds became darker and less uniform in tone, with gradations that created an illusion of depth.

Paintings of narrative scenes also appear in illustrated manuscripts. In Burma the medium employed at the court, especially during the Konbaung period (1752–1885), was the *parabaik*, a folding book made of specially prepared paper [113]. Some depict scenes from the life of the Buddha, while others show donations made by members of the royal family to the monastery, historical processions and events [112], or scenes of entertainments at court. Most surviving manuscripts date from after 1857 when the Burmese capital was moved to Mandalay. The style echoes that of mural paintings, with the outlines of figures drawn first and then filled with generally flat areas of colour. A sense of perspective is conveyed by overlapping figures and there is a tendency either to depict scenes from above or to include multiple perspectives. Each spread of the book contains a complete scene with a border around it, usually with a narrow yellow panel below containing a brief explanatory text. Later examples include a high horizon and shading of figures, perhaps reflecting European influence.

Another type of Burmese manuscript, which dates back at least to the fourteenth century and probably earlier, is the book of religious texts on prepared palm leaves, sandwiched between wooden boards and held together by a cord or pin [114]. The boards are often embellished with gilt or lacquer and the whole book wrapped with a long narrow tablet-woven ribbon. These

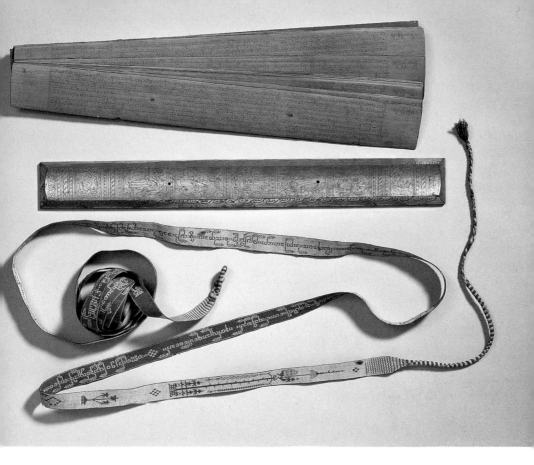

ribbons are works of art in themselves, often with verses written in Pali and a dedicatory phrase woven into the band. The texts on the palm-leaf pages are incised with a metal stylus, with lamp black rubbed into the incisions.

The traditions of Theravada art are remarkably consistent throughout mainland Southeast Asia, reflecting a desire for orthodoxy and a conception of artistic representation as essentially a teaching medium. While sponsors of Buddhist art could thereby gain merit, the embellishment of temples never became excessively ornate, nor did artists seek to make their mark by introducing innovations. Buddhism remains a central element in the art of mainland Southeast Asia, both in traditional media and in forms that have emerged in more recent times, reflecting the persisting strength of the religion and its position at the core of mainland culture.

114 Burmese religious manuscript between wooden boards with a tablet-woven braid. 60 × 512 × 40 mm.

Chapter 5   Islamic conceptions

The presence of Islamic ideas in the art of Southeast Asia has been less visible than those of Hinduism and Buddhism. Where the religion took hold, chiefly in the Malay Peninsula, the archipelago and the north coast of Borneo, it was philosophical and aesthetic ideas rather than iconography that had the most profound impact on material culture. This was primarily because visual symbolism in Islam operates in many ways differently from in other creeds. Muslim artists tend to deal with abstract ideas, which are suggested rather than openly expressed, alluded to in patterns and designs that form a kind of graphic symbolism. The prohibition on idolatry, derived from the Hadith, or traditions, which set down that living creatures should not be depicted, is one key factor in this. The singularity of God in Islam and the insistence that neither his prophet, Mohammad, nor any other being should be portrayed, greatly limited the range of subjects within the Muslim artistic repertoire. Thus there was no counterpart in Islamic art to the narrative scenes from the Hindu epics or the lives of the Buddha found in the reliefs and murals of the region. Similarly, the practice of venerating images of deceased rulers became largely defunct in those places where Islam was the dominant religious force.

Precisely how Islam reached Southeast Asia is not entirely clear, though it is likely that it arrived in different ways and at different times in various parts of the region. Traders from Islamicized parts of India, such as Gujerat, and from the Chinese coast probably first brought the faith to those parts where international trade was most active. Links with the Middle East are indicated in early texts, suggesting that Muslim traders were visiting the region not long after the adoption of Islam by the Arab peoples in the seventh century. Barus in northwest Sumatra seems to have had very early connections with the Arab world, itself linked by trade to the Mediterranean and the Indian subcontinent by sea, and through Central Asia and beyond to China by overland

115 Embroidered cover for a baby, Palembang, Sumatra. The smaller piece is placed above the child's head, its Qur'anic script invoking protection for the infant. 255 × 380 mm.

116 Tomb of Kajeng Ratu Ibu, the wife of King Cakraningrat I, at the royal cemetery of the Cakraningrat family, Arosbaya, Bangkalan, Madura. The image of the mountain has retained its significance in Islamic art in Indonesia. 17th century

routes. It seems that by the time Marco Polo was returning to Europe from China at the end of the thirteenth century, some parts of northern Sumatra had already converted to Islam. However, Islam does not appear to have gained large numbers of followers there until the fourteenth and fifteenth centuries.

The earliest centres of Islam in the region, in north and eastern Sumatra, were followed by coastal settlements in the Sulu archipelago, Brunei, the north coast of Java, and the northeast coast of peninsular Malaysia. Foreign traders who married local women may have established some of these communities; others were probably at least in part composed of Southeast Asian sailors and traders who had converted in the course of their travels. A tombstone found at Gresik in eastern Java and another in Brunei have been dated by some commentators to the eleventh century. If this is correct it is likely that these were isolated instances; the first documentary evidence of Muslim settlements in Gresik dates to the fifteenth century. By then there were Muslim graves even at Trowulan in the centre of the Majapahit kingdom in eastern Java.

Javanese legend tells of nine *walis*, or saints who were the first to propagate the faith there. Some are described as being of Chinese descent, at least in part, and the towns of the north coast

of Java show much evidence of Chinese culture alongside or perhaps as part of Islamic influence. The growing prosperity of Islamic trading centres probably aided the spread of the religion, and local kings and rulers began to convert, many taking the Islamic title of Sultan. After Majapahit had fallen into decline in the fifteenth century under pressure from the Islamic state of Demak, on the north coast of Java, Malacca, on the west coast of peninsular Malaysia, became the major power in the region. It was probably during this period that Malay began to take its place as the dominant language of trade for the whole region. When Malacca was conquered by the Portuguese in the early sixteenth century, the sultanate of Aceh in northern Sumatra, which had long been a major stronghold of Islam, began to assert its influence. However, it was never able to exert control over large areas, and by this time European incursions had become the major dimension in the struggle for power in maritime Southeast Asia.

Attempts from the seventeenth century onward by the Dutch and English East India Companies to wrest control from local rulers and to gain a monopoly of trade led to a strengthening of political alliances between many of the sultanates. Although they were never able to present a united front against European interference, Islam became a uniting cultural force. In much of what later became Malaysia and Indonesia, European influences on artistic expression were minimal, while Islamic modes of expression gained general currency, albeit integrated into the pre-existing idiom [116].

Until relatively recent times, Islam in Southeast Asia tended to accommodate many older beliefs and social practices. One reason may have been the original influence of Sufi teachers, whose emphasis was on the spiritual and mystical aspects of the religion. Where these men obtained influence at court, their ideas were subsumed into a culture that already placed much importance on magic, ritual and spirituality. Beauty in nature was regarded as a reflection of the innate beauty of the God who had created it. Art was used to communicate basic concepts of Islamic philosophy, especially in an attempt to help the individual to reach a harmonious understanding of the universe. Existing practices such as the retreat from worldly life, meditation and fasting in order to reach unity with the absolute were perfectly in keeping with Sufi thought. Understandings of cosmology were also to a considerable degree shared between old and new faiths, and in art, images such as the endless knot and the mandala, the appreciation of symmetry and balance, and the expression of the

117 Mesjid Agung, the great mosque at Banten, built in 1556 by Sultan Maulana Jusuf. The minaret is 30 metres tall.

118 Traditional mosque with tiered roof, Palopo, Sulawesi.

sense of an all-pervading life force were compatible with Islamic aesthetic principles.

In architecture, this change in religion would not have brought immediately striking changes. The requirements for a Muslim house of worship are few, and could be accommodated in existing architectural structures. Most timber mosques in the early period were adapted either from the pavilions in *kratons,* or palaces, or, in village communities, from the public meeting houses, or *balai*. These open buildings, designed on a square plan, normally consisted of columns supporting a hipped roof. As with some vernacular architecture, the centralized roof often consisted of more than one tier, allowing a louvre for ventilation between the levels [118]. The columns in traditional houses in many parts of the region carry symbolic significance, related for example to conceptions of life force or kinship structures. The pillar is also a central symbol in Islam, associated with not incompatible meanings. The multi-tiered roof had served in Hindu temples both as a canopy sheltering the central image, and as an upward channel connecting the deity with the heavens. In Islam, the deity was invisible and unrepresentable, but this vertical emphasis was retained, reinterpreted in terms of access to the gateway to paradise beyond the sky, which was itself referenced in the empty space below the central peak of the roof. Although the *kiblat*, prayer toward Mecca, provides the spiritual thrust of Islam, this is indicated within the mosque by the *mihrab*, a niche in the wall, and is not necessarily expressed in the orientation of mosque buildings. However, the orientation of the structure toward the kiblat is clearly evident in, for example, the late fifteenth-century mosque at the Kasepuhan kraton in Cirebon, north Java, where it is at an angle to other buildings in the royal complex, which are aligned with the cardinal points.

The earliest grand mosque on the north coast of Java was at Demak, founded in 1478, while those at Cirebon, Jepara, Kudus and Gresik were all built within the following hundred years. Such early mosques were often on sites that were already sacred, sometimes recycling materials from existing structures. The mosque in Mantingan near Jepara, which originally dates from

119 The lotus motifs on this medallion at the 16th-century mosque in Mantingan reveal the continuity of symbolism from earlier periods. On the reverse of some of the medallions are carvings from an earlier, Hindu monument.

1559, seems to have been built partly of stones that had been decorated on their reverse in pre-Islamic times with carvings of scenes from the Ramayana [119]. Many features of Hindu temples were retained in these great mosques. Those built at the Kasepuhan palace at Cirebon, at Demak, Kadilangu and Banten all retain the multi-tiered roofs so characteristic of the Hindu architecture of Bali and of buildings from the East Javanese period [117]. At the Sunyaragi pleasure garden and the kratons in Cirebon as well as at Sendang Duwur [124] the split gate (*candi bentar*) of monuments from the classical Hindu period in East Java is also in evidence. Courtyards and *gopuras* also refer back to Hindu forms.

It was not until the nineteenth century that architectural styles from elsewhere in the Islamic world became widespread in the Southeast Asian region. This may have happened partly in reaction to European domination, as well as asserting the connection with the international world of Islam. In some parts of what is now Malaysia, local rulers were encouraged to build by the British colonial regime, and this gave rise to a number of palaces and mosques in styles containing echoes of Indian and Middle Eastern architecture [120]. Features such as domes and minarets were inspired by both Mughal and Turkish examples; other elements were derived from colonial models of the British Raj. Although some ceramic tilework was applied and a few mosques were embellished with decorative patterning in the brickwork, the elaborate geometric surface ornamentation found elsewhere in the Muslim world is still rare in Southeast Asia, where space and light are key.

120 The Jami Masjid in Kuala Lumpur, built in 1897, with minarets, walled courtyards and bands of red and white brick, demonstrates Malay connections with international styles of Islamic architecture.

121 One of the bathing pools at Taman Sari, the 'water palace', a place of contemplation in the pleasure garden at Yogyakarta Built by the first sultan, Mangkubumi, in 1765.

122 The shape of this jewelled Malay tobacco box, *chelepa*, refers to the eight-petalled lotus flower, a common feature of Malay art and an example of the syncretism of artistic elements to be found in the region. Trengganu, Malaysia. Royal heirloom, probably 18th-century.

123 Detail of a cotton batik skirt cloth in the '*megamendung*' design from Cirebon. The realization of the cloud motif is derived from Chinese styles, said to have entered the repertoire after the local ruler married a Mongolian princess. Its resonance is strongly Islamic, however, which may account for its longevity in Cirebon designs. Made at the Gunung Jati workshop, Trusmi, Cirebon, 1990s. 1040 × 240 mm.

Where art has been used in the service of Islam it has been predominantly to celebrate God's creation. The images of fruits and flowers, foliage and tendrils that had in Hindu-inspired art provided background to a narrative, now became the subject matter. These were manifestations of God's handiwork, even of God's essence. Depictions of animals and birds, on the other hand, became less evident than before. In the past they had often been camouflaged, half hidden, but under Islamic influence this tendency was emphasized. While representations of living creatures have never been entirely eliminated, in many cases their forms have become so obscured, so allusive, that they are barely visible. In the intricate woodcarvings that decorate the houses and palaces built by and for Muslims, floral and vegetal motifs predominate, as they do on the richly embossed, engraved and incised works in silver, bronze and gold of Malay metalworkers [122]. In this the difference between these artefacts and those of their Hindu predecessors was not a great one, and in many cases the difference is barely discernible. Sometimes, at least to the untutored eye, only the absence of the figures of *apsaras* (nypmhs), astrological motifs or figures from the Hindu epics distinguishes the work of Islamic artists from that of their counterparts on the Buddhist mainland.

One medium in which Hindu forms were given a new Islamic interpretation was batik, one of the arts traditionally accorded the

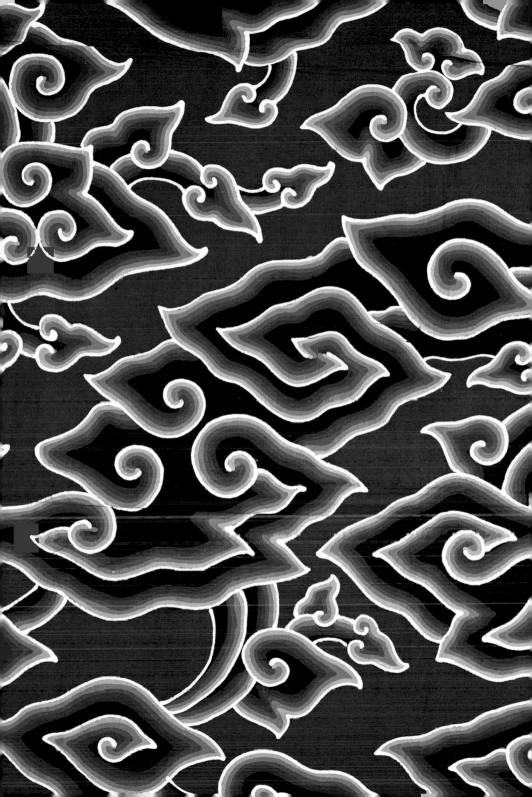

epithet *alus* in Central Java, denoting its status as a fine art. The origins of batik, the art of decorating cloth with a wax-resisted dye, are obscure. It is likely that simple forms of batik had been produced in the Javanese countryside for centuries before batik was introduced to the courts. When that occurred is also uncertain, but by the time of Sultan Agung, the great seventeenth-century ruler of the court of Mataram, several designs were reserved for royal use. While batik designs have not remained static, such proscriptions have preserved some of the old designs, and these are widely used today in the more egalitarian state of Indonesia. It is clear that the origins of many royal batik motifs lie in Hinduism. The *megamendung* cloud design relates both to the Chinese heavenly emperor and to the Hindu god Indra, enthroned on his mountain in the clouds [123]. Cloud motifs also occur repeatedly in Cirebon monumental architecture, for example at the gateway to the palace. The image of Mount Meru and of the other mountain ranges encircling the world occurs in many of the dark brown, blue and white patterns of the royal courts of Central Java, as does a range of motifs referring to the mount of Vishnu, the man-eagle Garuda. Other design elements signify Islamic referents more clearly. For example, in the batik of the court of Cirebon, scenes of the pleasure garden, or *taman arum*, are prominent, recalling the four gardens of Paradise described in the Qur'an and depicted in carpets of Persia and India, as well as the actual meditation gardens [121] where sultans would seek a state of *Sunya Ragi*, in which their spirits would merge with the universe.

Another batik motif that derives from both Islamic and Hindu traditions is the *peksinagaliman*, a compound mythological beast fusing elements from various sources. It has the neck of the naga, nowadays often described as a Chinese dragon, the trunk of an elephant, seen as a reference to Hinduism, and the wings of the Bouraq, the creature with the head of a woman, the body of a horse and the wings and tail of a peacock, that carried the prophet Mohammad to heaven [125]. Such iconographic and religious syncretism is characteristic of Cirebon art. Both inside the royal palace and outside the royal apartments, Chinese plates and blue tiles from Delft decorated with religious scenes have been set into the walls, while elsewhere are motifs from the Middle East such as the basket design. The Great Mosque at Cirebon also includes motifs such as a stylized *kala-makara* above and below the *mimbar* (pulpit), and at the mihrab a lotus symbol, which in Islamic Cirebon is reinterpreted as symbolizing the saying *Hayyin ila Ruhin*, or 'life without soul'.

In Islamic art, the arrangement of elements can be more significant than the elements themselves, and this is also evident in batik work. The borders of the batiks from Malay Jambi, for example, generally consist of three bands containing scrolls of leaves and tendrils [127]. This design is derived from the endless vine, which in China as well as in the Islamic world referred to the idea of time passing in regular repeating cycles. In China the flowers and fruits that 'spring' from the vine were seen as references to human offspring, though it is not clear whether such readings were current in Southeast Asia.

Another feature recurrent in Islamic designs is the way a pattern often seems to disappear behind the border that encloses it, the motifs at the edges cut off as if they are present but invisible behind the frame. As with the vine, these elements also convey notions of eternity and infinity that occur repeatedly in Islamic thought. Regular patterns which could have been arranged to fit neatly within the frame are denied the completion demanded by the eye, forcing the observer to attend to the reality beyond surface appearance. This combination of the sense of the finite with that of the infinite invokes the coincidental presence of the temporal with the spiritual. The main body of the cloth may also be divided into smaller and smaller segments, so that it is impossible to pinpoint the boundaries between one design element and the next. This is characteristic of Islamic pattern, and represents a graphic expression of indefinability, or what has been called 'the dissolution of matter'. It occurs not only in Malay

124 One of the gateways at Sendang Duwur, the burial place in 1585 of the Muslim saint Sunan Sendang, near Paciran in East Java. The rock motifs and pavilions above the gateway, as well as the wing shapes, are reminiscent of those found in Javanese batik, and probably have a similar significance. The symbolism of the wings, which echo the wing shapes found on batu Aceh tombstones, may relate to spiritual flight.

125 Detail of batik cloth from Cirebon depicting the *Taman Arum Sunyragi*, the 'perfumed gardens' where the sultan would meditate. Rocky landscapes were constructed in such gardens; the lions and peksinagaliman are imaginary.

126 Gold-thread brocade, or *songket*, is found throughout the Malay world. This fine example is from Brunei. 2042 × 1072 mm.

127 Batik shawl, or *selendang*, from Jambi in Sumatra. The yellow and brown dyes are used in such a way as to produce the effect of gold against the blue ground, gold being a favourite element in Malay art. 940 × 1920 mm.

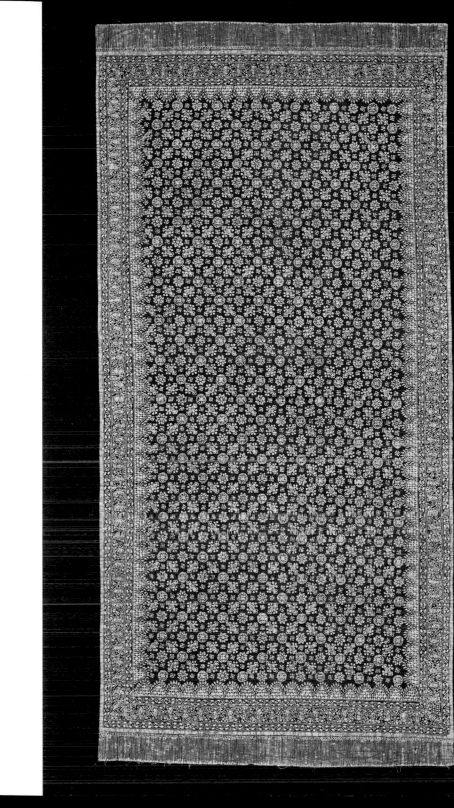

brocades [126] and the batiks of Jambi but also in the better-known batiks from Java and neighbouring Madura. Indeed, in Madura, the names given to batik designs almost invariably identify what a western observer might regard as the background 'filling' rather than the larger foreground elements of birds or flowers.

The Javanese approach to the interpretation of a piece of batik reveals much about Islamic aesthetics. Textile patterns are regarded as having not meanings but *sifat*, a word imported from Arabic that loosely translates as 'character', 'nature' or 'form'. The motif may refer to the essence of an object but does not represent it; rather the object suggested is itself suggestive of something else, a philosophical concept or a feeling. This allusiveness can only be appreciated by those with religious and spiritual knowledge. Different observers are expected to read a pattern at different levels, and patterns carry a multitude of shifting ideas which may depart from one another, overlap or merge into one. As a gateway to ideas and feelings, or *rasa*, art can transport the discerning beholder beyond the outer mundane world of material things toward an inner abstract reality.

A similar tendency to obliqueness is evident in the calligraphic batiks produced in Sumatra as well as in coastal centres of northern Java [128]. In some of these, it is possible to read phrases taken from the Qur'an, clearly intended to be legible to those who used the cloths. Most of these are likely to have been worn as head coverings by holy men, leaders and those engaged in the struggle against the Dutch, or laid over the biers of those who identified with or had died in that struggle. Some were carried as banners and echo the design of banners used by the Ottoman army, and there were talismanic vests employing similar designs, which again may well have been modelled on those worn elsewhere in the Islamic world. In these contexts, the script carried a clear meaning, whether or not the observer could read it, identifying the bearer, the wearer or the deceased with Islam. Depictions of the holy sword, the Dhu'l-Faqar, which had been given by Mohammad to his son-in-law Ali, would likewise be recognizable to most Muslims as would representations, often made from contorted script, of the lion of God, itself the symbol of Ali. Many other motifs on the calligraphic cloths, however, were much less accessible, both to outsiders and to lay people in the community. A motif based on the *tughra*, the emblematic signature of an Ottoman sultan, appears frequently in these cloths, and features today in handbooks of designs used by Islamic artists and calligraphers in the region. It may once have been recognized

as making explicit a link with the great overseas Islamic power. The symbol has been retained at least in part for its talismanic properties. Some inscriptions on these batiks consist of script so twisted and manipulated that it can barely be read at all. In some cases the script is written in mirror image, in others it is encoded. The power of other devices, such as magic squares, in which numbers were arranged according to a secret formula, seems to have lain precisely in their indecipherability to those who were not initiated.

The need to protect houses and people, especially at rites of passage, had been the motivating force behind much artistic production in pre-Islamic Southeast Asia, and it continued to be of importance in a world filled with *jinns*, spirits that could be benign or malignant. Where previously inscriptions in Sanskrit may have carried protective potency, now phrases taken from the Qur'an

128 The script in the diagonal bands of this batik headcloth is highly stylized. That in the corners is arranged symmetrically so that each corner mirrors another, which renders the script illegible but the cloth more powerful. Indonesia. 870 × 920 mm.

were brought into play. In Cirebon, art played a major part in the articulation of religious ideas, and the talismanic properties of the holy scriptures were invoked in a number of media. The artists and artisans seem to have belonged to *tariqats*, Sufi brotherhoods consisting of artistic communities. Villages specializing in a particular craft were founded by religious and artistic leaders whose graves were tended and treated with respect for generations. Mystical philosophies are often concealed in abstract forms in the designs of their artworks, accessible only to members of the guild that produced them.

Artistic traditions at Cirebon continue to thrive, among them the art of painting on glass [129]. Mosques were popular subjects of glass paintings, which were sold to be hung as domestic decorations and protective talismans, by itinerant artists. Figures from the wayang shadow theatre also provided subject matter, especially figures from the Mahabharata such as Kresna and Arjuna, as well as the god Batara Guru and Vishnu's mount, Garuda. Although these figures are primarily Hindu in association, in glass paintings they were often formed from letters spelling out phrases from the Qur'an, a perfect melding of the two religions. While other parts of the pictures were painted in dark colours, the Arabic script was drawn in gold or bronze paint, the words shining out from the background. The pictures were regarded as being suffused with a protective force derived both from the characters and from the texts. This visual moulding of Hindu motifs into an Islamic form is characteristic of the region but most clearly articulated in Cirebon. It is echoed in stories and legends telling of encounters between the two worlds, such as the story of Arjuna's visit to Mecca.

As in many other arts, the introduction of Islam did not result in fundamental changes to the design and decoration of weaponry. Cannons intended for the protection of the Muslim sultanates were cast by bronze-workers in various parts of the archipelago, especially northern Sumatra and Brunei. Their forms tended to echo those of Chinese cannon, with the main body shaped like a crocodile or dragon, the shot propelled from the creature's mouth. In Brunei, miniature cannon were used for many purposes, including the payment of bridewealth [130].

Daggers, as well as many other weapons, took a more prominent place in those cultures that embraced Islam. In the Sulu archipelago linking Borneo with the Philippines, knives developed features not found elsewhere in the region. The leaf-shaped blade of the *barung*, favoured by Tausug warriors, is unique, as is the

129 Glass painting of the Bouraq, the winged horse with a woman's face and peacock's tail which carried the prophet Mohammad to heaven.

kampilan, a weapon used by Muslims on mainland Mindanao, with a double-edged blade narrower at the hilt than at the tip. The influence may be as much from Spain as from the Islamic world, and the design of armour in the Philippines also owed much to European styles. However, body armour was sometimes embellished with the wing motif, probably derived from the motif adorning textile tunics worn into battle by Muslims, from the Ottoman Empire in the west to Java in the east.

The keris [131], whose origins in Java preceded the arrival of Islam, came into its own under the Muslim sultanate of Mataram. Nonetheless, the iconography bears little evidence of Islamic ideas. The undulating blade of one type of keris is often likened to the naga, and the hilt to a bird, whose form it often takes. The bird-serpent combination refers back to pre-Islamic ideas, with some hilts made in the shape of wayang heroes such as Bhima. Even so, the keris became inextricably linked with Islam. In the Philippines, for example, the keris is associated with all Muslim groups but no non-Muslim groups.

In Java one of the central features of a keris and an indicator of its quality is the *pamor*, the patterning with which the blade is decorated, sometimes referred to as damascening. Although the Indonesian pamor may be the result of influence from the Islamic world it is not produced by the process of damascening (named

after Damascus, where the technique was widely practised). In Java the effect is produced by the process of pattern welding, which Indonesian smiths may have discovered while attempting to replicate the damascening seen on imported weapons. In the processes of manufacture and in the meanings associated with the keris, Islamic understandings become clearly apparent. In Java, fasting and religious thanksgiving ceremonies have long been important activities which the keris-maker must perform before starting work. These are now firmly located within an Islamic framework, and fit within recognized liturgical parameters. The power with which a keris is imbued is regarded as a gift from God.

A similar set of beliefs is at work on the Indonesian island of Bima, where the maker of a keris traditionally goes through a period of fasting and prayers before commencing his work. He is expected to be aware of *kebe*, a term derived from Arabic which refers to the supernatural power to cause harm to an enemy or otherwise alter future events. Another Islamic concept that comes into play is *firasa*, the ability to discern a person's temperament from their appearance. This is an important skill because the

130 Double-barrelled miniature cannon of *mariam* type mounted on a four-wheeled carriage, with a third barrel between the two main ones. Behind this is a figure of a dog, standing with its mouth open. 154 × 280 mm.

design of a keris should be in keeping with the character of the man who is to use it.

An Islamic perspective often underlies the way a weapon is 'read'. In Aceh, it is often suggested that the shape of the various parts of the *rencong*, the favoured weapon among Acehnese men, depict the phrase '*Bismillah*', or 'in the name of Allah'. This is the opening of the phrase '*Bismillah al-rahman al-rahim*', 'in the name of God, the Merciful, the Compassionate', which occurs at the start of each sura of the Qur'an. The curves of the hilt and the blade, together with the shape of the decoration at the base of the hilt, the tip of the blade and the base of the scabbard are said to form its component letters. Such readings typify the Islamic search for the presence of God in every aspect of the world, whether in nature or in the handiwork of humans, thus reinforcing the identification with Islam in every part of life.

Clothing was one of the areas of material culture most influenced by the new religion. Although Chinese custom may have had some impact, it was from Islam that the practice of covering the upper body with tailored garments was introduced. Wearing trousers was also largely the result of influence from Persia and the Arab world, as the names used for these garments testify. The Malay sultanates and the sultanate of Aceh may have modelled their court ceremonies and the costumes worn at them

131 Nine-waved keris and sheath, with a hilt in the form of a *rakshasha* demon. The top of the sheath has a large *kala* head mask in gold, with 'diamond' eyes. The gold cover of the sheath is decorated with intricate floral and foliate designs, with swastikas and a *garuda* and *singa* design between the bands. The keris was presented to a Scottish captain, John Brown, by the Sultan of Madura, in 1816. 585 × 175 mm.

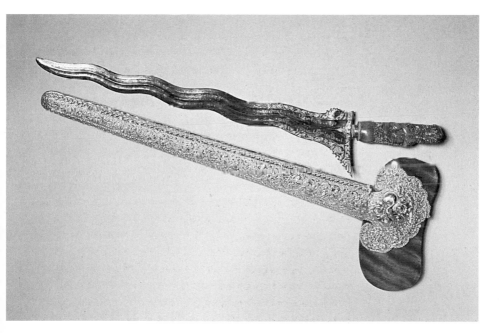

at least in part on those of the Mughal and Ottoman courts. Techniques for costume decoration also owed much to ideas and examples brought back from the *hajj*, the annual pilgrimage to Mecca in Arabia. Items from the holy sites were imbued with supernatural power and it is not surprising that styles and materials served as models for local production. Malay culture in particular was strongly affected, with gold strips couched onto backings of velvet or silk becoming a regular feature in ceremonial costume and still used for hangings and cushions placed around the bridal throne and over doorways, the gold sometimes forming phrases from the Qur'an [132]. Gauze veils and head coverings from other parts of the Islamic world, especially those decorated with silver strips, were also admired, and when they could not be obtained from overseas they were produced locally.

Another area on which Islam had a profound effect was in relation to burial practices. From at least the fourteenth century, graves were marked with stones; some were produced locally, at sites in Brunei, eastern Java and northern Sumatra, while others were imported from other parts of the Islamic world including

132 Detail of a Malay hanging for a doorway in couched gold and pearls on velvet, depicting the flowers and fruit of the tree of paradise. Central Sumatra.

Cambay in India, and China. Inscribed gravestones known in peninsular Malaysia as *batu Aceh, or* Aceh stones, occur throughout Islamic Southeast Asia, in the Sulu archipelago, along the Bornean coast, in the Malay Peninsula as well as on Indonesian islands such as Java and Sumatra. Whether all these stones originated in Aceh is not known, though it is quite possible; the practice of importing gravestones continues to this day in the peninsula.

The earliest batu Aceh were produced in the fifteenth century and were made from pairs of stone slabs, one as a headstone and the other for the foot of the grave [135]. Often tombstones were left blank, but finer examples are carved on both sides, usually with a frame containing an inscription giving the name of the deceased and either a quotation from the Qur'an, the Shahadah (the Islamic profession of faith) or sometimes lines of Sufi verse, usually relating to the transience of life on earth. Some of the examples found in cemeteries in the Pasai area of northern Sumatra show stylistic links with existing traditions of carving on the island. One of the most beautiful of such early tombstones commemorates the burial of a woman around 1436 [133]: the headstone is carved in sharp relief, with gently curved parallel lines terminating in spirals that divide the outer panels of stylized script from the central panel with a rosette at its heart, and wave and dentate strips embellishing the base. In a contemporary stone of more classic design, the curved crown of the stone is finished with a flat top, with wings known as subang or 'earrings' at each shoulder [134]. An elegantly framed panel is divided horizontally into four sections, each with tall lines of boldly carved Naskhi script rising from it. Above the panel is a smaller one, in the shape of an upturned heart. This type of design is characteristic of batu Aceh found elsewhere in the region.

Later examples of batu Aceh are carved into pillars, often sloping outward as they rise, and with eight facets resembling a lotus bud. Sometimes the tops of the facets are curved like the top of a petal. Almost all batu Aceh contain some part of the lotus plant in their design, revealing the syncretism of artistic styles so prevalent in Southeast Asian art. Other motifs such as rosettes and vines are more likely to have derived from Islamic tradition, the former perhaps referring to heaven, eternity and unity.

The most important expression of Islamic ideals is in the Qur'an, and in the calligraphy in which it is written. The significance of writing is emphasized many times in the Qur'an, and writing was regarded as having a divine origin. For this reason,

133 The rounded shoulders and the flat-topped crown of this tombstone relate its design to that of contemporary stones. The spiral forms are familiar in pre-Islamic art, as are the rope or wave motifs on the base. The rosette or star motif at the centre is frequently employed in Islamic work as is the arrangement of script to fill the available space. Pasai area of north Sumatra, 1436 or 1437.

134 The *subang*, or earring, shape at the shoulders became a characteristic element of batu Aceh, as did the division of the script into neat horizontal panels. Forms commonly found in Islamic art are the knots and the cloud-shaped terminals on the base. Pasai area of north Sumatra, 1438.

the most beautiful manifestations of Islam in Southeast Asian art are depictions of the word, whether carved in stone or wood, embroidered or dyed into cloth, engraved or chased in metal or, perhaps most importantly, written in ink on paper. The most elaborately decorated work in Malay manuscript art is devoted to copies of the Qur'an, with chapter headings and colophon given the most attention, often with strongly delineated frames containing repeated vegetal and floral patterns.

The oldest surviving Malay manuscripts date back to the early sixteenth century. Beautifully decorated letters written in the Malay language were used throughout the Southeast Asian archipelago for communication with other Malay speakers, with those in other parts of Asia and with Europeans [136]. Traditional Malay guides to letter writing, *kitab terasul*, set down the conventions to be followed in the forms of address, literary style and phrases appropriate for particular occasions or recipients, according to their rank and status. There was also advice on the folding of letters, the positioning of the seal and so on. But there were no set rules on the decoration, and court scribes and illuminators were able to embellish them with their own variations of elegant calligraphy and ornamental flourishes.

135 A group of tombstones in situ at a cemetery in the Pasai area of north Sumatra, showing the arrangement of pairs. Stones of this type without *subang* are widely found in the Aceh area as well as in Pasai, and were exported from there to other parts of the Malay world.

136 Letter from Sultan Ahmad of
Terengganu to Baron van der
Capellen in Batavia. 1824. It is
written in ink and gold on paper,
with a lamp-black seal. 498 ×
383 mm.

137 Islamic manuscript traditions
in Southeast Asia are rarely include
figures, but Java is an exception. In
this scene, Prince Selarasa pays
obeisance to the holy man Kiai Nur
Sayid, who has been fasting in the
wilderness for so long that a vine
has grown up around him.

The traditional forms of Malay letters owe much to influence from India, Persia and Turkey. Ottoman calligraphers may have been at work in the court of Aceh, where some of the finest were written. Persian influence is evident not just in the form of the wording and the arrangement of the texts on the page, but also in the aesthetic qualities of the manuscripts. Scribes were careful not to leave gaps at the ends of lines, filling any spaces with additional pen strokes. The balance between the proportions of the text block and the rest of the page was also important, with the top third of the paper and a large margin on the right-hand side normally left blank. Only the most important letters were decorated, but of those that were, the embellishment was lavish. The principal material for this was gold, which connoted wealth and majesty, while elaborate borders and scattered flowers typical of Malay applied art are frequent features.

Despite their highly developed calligraphy, Malay manuscripts were rarely as illustrated as those of the Javanese [137], who felt less constrained by Islamic disapproval of the depiction of human figures and whose texts were often accompanied by scenes derived from Hindu and secular sources. In Malay manuscripts, with the exception of chancery letters, the emphasis tended to be on the text itself. In most cases, the seals authorizing the letters are their most beautiful element – usually made of silver [138]. Most royal Malay seals were round, though some, like those of the first three sultans of Pontianak, were octagonal in shape. Circular seals were often surrounded by eight peripheral petal shapes reminiscent of the lotus flower. Occasionally there were four, twelve, or sixteen such petals and in Aceh, some seals had seven or nine. The central circle generally contained the name of the reigning monarch, as was the case with the seals of the sultans of Aceh. Around this central circle the Acehnese seals showed the names of eight previous sultans, contained in eight smaller circles, an arrangement inspired by the seal of the Mughal emperors. Within and surrounding these shapes the seal makers engraved the arabesque and foliate forms so typical of Malay art.

Despite the strength of Islam in parts of Southeast Asia and the significance accorded to items of material culture in the Malay and Javanese courts, Islamic principles are not always immediately apparent in the art works of the region. The effect of Muslim ideas on material forms was frequently subtle, and Islam had as much influence on the perspective from which art was viewed as it did on the forms themselves. While some new materials and techniques were introduced from other parts of the Islamic world,

it was largely in the interpretation of the relationship between the visible, material world and its invisible, spiritual counterpart that Islam played its part. Here, with the notable exception of the manifestation of the word of God, it was the invisible which was paramount.

Chapter 6   Chinese influence

Contact between China and Southeast Asia has left a significant
impression on the arts of the region, though one that is less
pronounced than that of India. Chinese styles and conceptual
patterns have tended to make their mark not on monumental
architecture, for example, but in less public media and generally in
works produced on a smaller scale. There is no doubt, however,
that Chinese influence is of long standing. A Chinese presence is
recorded in Southeast Asia from the third century AD, with China
maintaining a politically important position which, though it
fluctuated from time to time as a result of internal difficulties, did
not finally come to an end until the fifteenth century. In trade,
both before and during the period of European expansion, many
Southeast Asian rulers relied heavily on Chinese intermediaries
who, for example, transported forest products from upriver
regions for export overseas. Many of these Chinese merchants
became wealthy and the style of their architecture and
possessions seems to have impressed many local rulers, for there
is evidence of Chinese styles in the paraphernalia that fills many of
the region's royal palaces. Malay sultans at various times sent for
Chinese craftsmen such as woodcarvers, jewellers and experts in
lacquer production, employing them to make fine items to adorn
their palaces. Chinese techniques and designs were incorporated
into local traditions or new ones developed; Palembang
lacquerware, for example, is well known for its fine quality.

Mercantile patterns have also left their mark: traders from the
coastal regions of southern China continued to introduce ideas
and practices well into the modern age, especially in the islands.
These included some aspects of Islamic art discussed in the
previous chapter. Direct migration into the region, especially
during the late Qing dynasty (1644–1911), has established sizeable
Chinese minorities. In early times, male settlers in the many
Chinese communities that sprang up along the coastal towns of

139 The Khue Van Cac pavilion,
built in 1805 at the Temple of
Literature, Hanoi

Southeast Asia tended to marry and be assimilated into the local population. This resulted in a melding of cultural forms, both material and social, so that Chinese elements were often rearticulated first in hybrid and then in new forms of expression. In some places, such as the Straits Settlements of Singapore, Penang and Malacca, there has been a tendency for more recent Chinese newcomers to retain the culture of the homeland in greater part, and in these places the older buildings and many cultural artefacts retain a character that is distinctly Chinese.

There are also ancient ethnic links between China and the Southeast Asian region. Groups such as the Hmong, Shan and ethnic Tai, whose ancestors migrated into the region along its northern borders with China, share a cultural legacy with groups in the provinces of southwestern China; because of this, there are also some similarities between Southeast Asian arts and the motifs and designs of the artwork of Chinese peoples.

Nonetheless, the introduction of artistic influences from China can be largely seen as separate from this shared heritage. It dates back to the Bronze Age, and styles and motifs of late Zhou art (1027 BC to AD 221) can be seen in some art of the region. The Dong Son drums, for example, are part of a wider tradition of which extensive remains have been found in Yunnan. In most parts of the region Chinese involvement was geared more toward trade than territorial ambition, and influence on art resulted from relations of exchange rather than conquest. The chief exception was Vietnam, which was directly ruled by China from 111 BC to AD 979. Nevertheless, in early times the attitude of Southeast Asian rulers throughout the region toward their powerful neighbour in the north tended to be one of deference. Chinese chronicles record delegations from Southeast Asia, or Nanyang, bearing trade or tribute items to the Chinese court as far back as the third century AD, and by the fifth century Chinese emissaries were being sent in large numbers to various parts of the region. From China came luxury goods such as porcelain and silk, exchanged for ivory, feathers, dyestuffs and fragrant woods from the forests of island Southeast Asia. While the splendours of the Chinese court made a considerable impression on Southeast Asians, it was the merchandise, especially those goods traded in bulk, that left a more lasting legacy. Foremost among these were ceramics.

Fragments of Chinese ceramics dating back to the Eastern Han period (AD 25–220) have been found in island Southeast Asia, often in burials. The range of material, which includes plates and tiles, figurines and lidded boxes, indicates the considerable impact

140 Stoneware *kendi* decorated with lotus petals and leaves, flaming pearls and chrysanthemum flowers in blue underglaze. Hac Bac province, Vietnam. *c.* 1500. Height 120 mm.

141 Sukhothai celadon: stoneware bottle glazed in olive green, with an incised cloud collar-pattern on the shoulder showing Chinese influence, a band of waves below and vertical lines on the lower body. *c.* 1400. Height 157 mm.

of Chinese culture on architecture and on the domestic life of the wealthier citizens of the region. This happened over a wide area: ceramics from the Tang and Sung dynasties are found in abundance throughout the region, testifying to an active mercantile relationship. The form and decoration of some of this material was adapted to local taste, and Chinese styles were also imitated in local materials. It is likely that the shape of the spouted water containers known as *kendi*, for example, was influenced by imported Chinese examples [140].

The techniques and materials of Chinese wares also provided a model for Southeast Asian potters to follow. In the Sukhothai kingdom in Thailand, for example, new firing and glazing techniques appeared at the start of the fourteenth century alongside motifs that undoubtedly owed their origin to China. It is possible that these were learned from Chinese craftsmen accompanying a mission returning to Sukhothai after offering tribute to the Chinese court. Certainly the styles of painted decoration on the wares produced at Sukhothai and Sawankhalok at this time, with dark strokes brushed onto a light background, echo the styles of painted wares made for local use in northern China. However, although the designs were copied, they were achieved in Thailand by using iron-black underglaze rather than

142 Sawankhalok figurines representing a widow with a fan; a woman with a baby; a male servant holding a jug; and a maid. Note the betel quid in the cheeks. Heights 81–115 mm.

cobalt as in China, which suggests that if there was direct influence, it occurred before the fourteenth century, when cobalt underglaze was incorporated into commercial production in China by the Yuan and later the Ming. A similar influence seems to have been at work in ceramics produced in Annam at around the same time, possibly through contact between Sukhothai and Annam, but more likely as a result of the simultaneous arrival of Chinese craftsmen in both these places. Nevertheless, the ceramics in these production centres often took distinctive local forms. The miniature figurines of humans and animals produced by Sawankhalok potters, for example, used as offerings to the spirits of ancestors, are unmistakable [142].

Khmer ceramics of this period were on the whole influenced far less by Chinese wares, which were nonetheless imported in some quantity. Locally manufactured earthenware pots were used for cooking, but the indigenous manufacture of glazed ceramics was limited. Best known are the containers for lime, one of the key ingredients of betel chew. In Cambodia the lime pots were often made in the shape of birds or animals, such as owls and elephants [143]. Khmer potters also produced religious vessels and figurines, architectural pieces such as tiles and finials, and items for domestic use. Most were made of coarse clay, usually with thin brown or green glazes.

One of the most striking elements of Chinese ceramics to find its way into the Southeast Asian repertoire was the celadon glaze, green in colour but melting into a grey or blueish tinge [141]. Celadon had been a feature of Chinese ceramics since the tenth century AD but appeared first in Thai ceramics in the thirteenth

143 Three Khmer stoneware lime pots from the Angkorian period, in the form of a brown-glazed smiling rabbit; brown-glazed smiling cat; and pale green-glazed frowning cat. Heights 120 mm; 100 mm; 95 mm.

century at Sawankhalok. It is possible that it was brought there by potters from China, though Vietnamese potters may also have travelled to Thailand at this time. The Thai wares differ from those of Chekiang province in eastern China, the most likely Chinese source, in that the glaze is thinner, more brittle and the surface less oleaginous. In Sawankhalok celadons, the decoration was usually achieved by incising a design into the body with a knife before glazing. Motifs echoed Chinese designs: the peony and the chrysanthemum were both popular and moulded rims were often formed into the shapes of lotus petals.

The use of ceramic elements in architecture seems to have begun at Sukhothai at around the same period [144]. This too is likely to have been a Chinese introduction, though Cambodian kilns also produced small architectural pieces in the thirteenth century. The lack of sandstone in northern central Thailand may have been a factor in encouraging the development of decorative architectural elements in ceramic. Freestanding sculptures, especially of guardian figures, finials, ridge caps and roof supports

144 Pair of stoneware naga finials from Sawankhalok, Sukhothai period, with brown and white glaze. Height 667 mm.

were made. Some of these were of considerable size, testimony to the skill of the Thai potters in firing ceramics at high temperature. They were finished with cream and green glazes, some decorated with incised or applied floral shapes.

The shapes of Vietnamese pottery were most clearly influenced by Chinese styles during the period of Chinese rule, from the first century BC to the tenth century AD. Even so, there were differences. Although the Vietnamese adopted the Chinese burial practice of interring miniature items with the body, this did not include ceramic human figures as were made for this purpose in China. The Vietnamese began to glaze ceramics around the first century BC but these glazes were creamy white or ivory with

145 Covered stoneware jar with white glaze from the Thanh Hoa region, Vietnam. The upper rim is decorated with moulded lotus petals, while the lid and body have carved foliate shapes accentuated with an iron-brown stain. 9th–10th century. Height 195 mm.

green splashes instead of the greens and golds used in China. Another difference was that in Vietnam there was a more prominent foot on the pottery compared with the Chinese style. One vessel seen in both China and Vietnam, however, was the twin-eared shallow cup, the similarity in form providing evidence of strong cultural interchange.

Under the Ly dynasty, which wrested control of Vietnam (or Dai Viet, as it was then known) from the Chinese in 1009, moulded ceramic dishes showed the influence of local silverware designs and also those of China. The brown and cream stoneware produced in Vietnam at this time [145] was influenced by Chinese ceramics, but the form of the pots and their decoration were distinctly Vietnamese. Motifs included a vegetal scroll, unlike Chinese motifs for the period. Jars often had out-turned lotus petal 'collars' under the top rim, with the clay typically a putty colour. Nor were the straight sides and open shape of Vietnamese jars features of Chinese material of the time.

Between the eleventh and fourteenth centuries Vietnamese potters were producing several types of 'black' wares. These had glazes with an iron content that had been increased to produce a colour that varied all the way from black to straw. Some of these may have been derivative of Chinese and Khmer wares, but others were more clearly indigenous in style. Typical of Vietnam was a pale celadon green produced by using a level of iron intermediate between that required for the pale straw colour and that needed for black. Another type was produced in a vivid green by means of either an iron or lead flux glaze with copper as the colourant.

The Vietnamese began to export beyond Dai Viet during the Tran dynasty, from the early fourteenth century. Vietnamese stonewares from this period have been found in Indonesia and the Philippines. Various forms of decoration were used. One involved motifs incised through the glaze, another was made with an iron underglaze, producing a brown effect. By the late thirteenth century an underglaze blue had been introduced, produced from cobalt, and this was used to decorate a range of wares exported in the fourteenth and fifteenth centuries. Monochrome blue wares were first produced in the fifteenth century in Vietnam for export to other parts of Southeast Asia. The kendi produced in Vietnamese kilns at this time were different in shape from Chinese kendi, with longer spouts and a compressed base.

In the mid-fifteenth century Vietnamese potters took advantage of the ban on overseas trade which the Ming emperor had imposed in China and set up in fierce competition in the

export trade. It was at this time that the finest Vietnamese blue and white underglaze ceramics were produced, in a style of ware that was manufactured in large quantities for shipping to the islands of Indonesia and the Philippines [146]. Water droppers and figures of court officials were included in these cargoes, as well as items with unglazed biscuit panels and ware enamelled in red, yellow and green. The trade continued into the sixteenth century and so some of these items found their way through the Dutch East India Company's office in Hanoi to the royal houses of Europe. Domestic ceramic ware included altar vessels combining biscuit fired elements with underglaze blue and another type made in cream and green with biscuit detailing. Vietnamese ceramics have continued to thrive, and are still produced today

Ceramic elements were used in Southeast Asian architecture wherever Chinese influence was strong. In Indonesia, for example, many Chinese temples were built as almost exact replicas of those found in mainland China, and ceramic features decorate the roofs of Chinese temples in Sumatra, Bali and along the north coast of Java [147]. The intermingling of Chinese iconography in early Islamic buildings in towns like Banten, Demak, Kudus, Jepara, Cirebon and Tuban is testimony to the presence of Muslim Chinese in Java from the late fifteenth century onward, a presence that also left its mark on palace architecture. The cloud motifs on

146 The blue and white trade-ware exported from Hanoi from the mid-fifteenth century contains echoes of the designs of the Chinese export-ware it replaced. The fish, waterweeds and band of peony flowers, as well as the cloud collar-band at the edge are all derived from Chinese models. Diameter 380 mm.

the gateway to the palace quarters at the Kasepuhan kraton in Cirebon and the wooden panels of the tombs of seventeenth-century rulers of Sumenep in Madura are purely Chinese [148]. Woodcarving designs produced in the nineteenth century at centres along the north Javanese coast and in Bali, as well as in Palembang and Jambi in eastern Sumatra, also echo the styles of southern China, especially on furniture and other items decorated with red lacquer and gilt.

Lacquer traditions in Southeast Asia almost certainly derive from Chinese lacquerwork, an art dating back over three thousand years. There is evidence that lacquerware was being made at Pyu monasteries from early times, although the earliest

147 Rooftop of a Chinese temple, Pekalongan, Java.

148 Cloud motifs on a gateway at the Kasepuhan kraton, Cirebon, West Java.

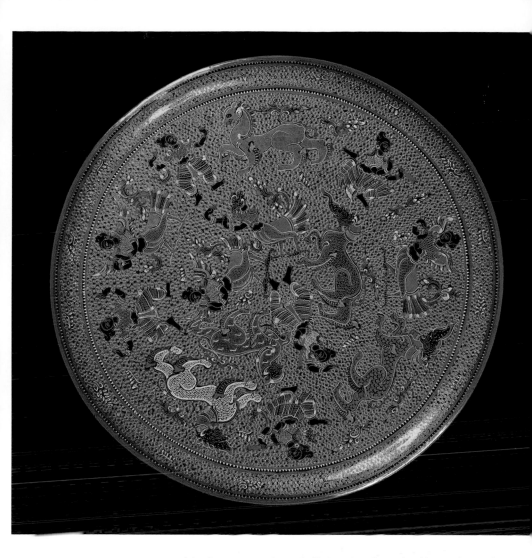

149 Lacquerware tray from Burma in the *yun* technique, with incised decoration in green, yellow and black on a red lacquer ground. The motifs include musicians, mythical beasts, and part-bird, part-human *kinaree*. 20th century. Diameter 418 mm.

surviving lacquerware items in Burma date from the thirteenth century. It is likely that the tradition was introduced through contact with the ethnic groups of Yunnan rather than directly from the Han Chinese, though this was probably not the case with moulded dry lacquer, of which there is no evidence in Thailand or Laos. Buddhist images made in this way were produced in Burma until the early twentieth century.

Styles of lacquerwork differ across the region. In Burma the most distinctive type, known as *yun* [149], involves the application of colour to patterns incised with a stylus into the outer layers of the lacquer. While the surface of the item may be brown, black or red, this technique allows for the decoration to be achieved in red, green, yellow and orange. In Thailand, the use of gold leaf to embellish lacquered items is more widespread, especially items used in the service of Buddhism. The application of gold leaf to Buddha images and other religious items is performed widely as a way of earning merit. Lacquered images are decorated with glass inlay in both Thailand and Burma, where this technique became popular in the eighteenth century.

Another technique of surface decoration that owes something to China is the use of mother-of-pearl to embellish a variety of receptacles. In Thailand this type of ornamentation is associated with the Ayutthaya and Bangkok periods, when it was employed in combination with lacquer on doors, furniture and receptacles used for making offerings. Both the technique and the materials differ, however, from those used in China. It may be that Thai artisans were introduced first to the finished product and worked back from it to discover the process for themselves, rather than being introduced to the Chinese methods of manufacture. In Thailand shapes cut from the concave turban shell were glued to the surface of the object, the spaces between later filled with sticky black lac. In China the shell used was much finer and more fragile, and it was set into indentations carved out from the surface of the item to be decorated. Lacquer was then applied, but in far lesser quantities than in the Thai version, since the spaces to be filled were much smaller. Among the most beautiful examples of Thai mother-of-pearl work are the doors created for Wat Borom Buddharam in Ayutthaya, and later removed to Bangkok after the city was sacked. Of similar quality are two renderings of the Buddha's footprint, one in Bangkok at Wat Chetupon on the feet of the reclining Buddha and the other formerly in Wat Phra Singh in Chiang Mai and now housed in the museum there.

150 Reconstructed dinh at Dinh Bang village, near Hanoi. Buildings of similar structure appear in decorations on some of the earliest Dong Son drums, and they seem to have retained a form which owes nothing to Chinese models. The function of the dinh, however, and the right to build one are closely tied to Chinese administrative and religious practices.

A millennium of direct rule also produced a considerable Chinese influence on Vietnamese architecture. Few buildings remain from the period before independence in the tenth century AD since they were for the most part constructed of wood, but Chinese influence can be clearly seen in more recent buildings, especially in imperial palaces and mausoleums, in which the bulk of the artistic vocabulary is Chinese. Even the *dinh*, or community houses, built in a largely indigenous style, show some Chinese influence [150]. Villages were traditionally granted the right to build a dinh by the Emperor, who also granted a charter and patron guardian; both the charter and the guardian spirit were housed in the dinh. This system continued after independence from China. The tendency toward a north–south orientation is a Chinese chartacteristic, as is the strong horizontal emphasis, with a broad roof supported by columns. The dominance of the roof, however, is an indigenous, rather than a Chinese characteristic, and the curved extremities of the roof are also local in origin. The traditional dinh was also built on piles, unlike nearly all other Vietnamese buildings, which are generally built on the ground in the Chinese way.

One of the earliest buildings still standing in Vietnam is the Temple of Literature in Hanoi, founded by the Emperor Ly Thanh Tong in the eleventh century and extended and restored at

151 The 11th-century One Pillar Pagoda in Hanoi.

various later periods [139]. In this complex are manifested some of the key components of Confucianism, a patriarchal moral code which advocates respect for one's elders and for the authority of the state. In the Temple of Literature, rows of stelae inscribed with the names of winners of the state Mandarin competition and set on the backs of tortoises (Chinese symbol of longevity) surround one of the five courtyards. These, with their low pavilions, are arranged in a north–south axis in an echo of Chinese aesthetic principles and practices, dominated by a sense of quiet harmony and order. A similar aesthetic sense is evoked by the One Pillar Pagoda (Chua Mot Cot), also originally established in Hanoi in the eleventh century by the same emperor and subsequently restored [151]. This unusual pagoda, set in a lily pond, symbolizes the lotus, rising from a sea of impurity and sorrow. Ceramic dragon figures ranged along the gently curved roof link the pagoda to the heavens.

Although many early Vietnamese royal palaces have been destroyed, those which remain from the nineteenth century clearly sought their inspiration in Chinese imperial models. In the imperial architecture of Vietnam, Chinese principles predominated. Buildings were set on a square ground plan, sometimes indented, enclosed within concentric walls and related to one another through linking courtyards in a north–south orientation. The roofs were covered with flat tiles or, at times of

152 Octagonal pavilion housing the stele of emperor Khai Dinh, a few kilometres upriver from Hue on the Perfume River. In the Honour Courtyard are rows of elephants, horses and mandarins, a feature copied from ancient Chinese tombs. Built between 1920 and 1931.

particularly strong Chinese influence, with half-round tiles in the Chinese style. The mausoleums of the Nguyen imperial dynasty (1802–1945), built along the Perfume River near Hue, similarly referred to Chinese imperial traditions, with dragon stairways and spirit roads lined with rows of figures of animals and court officials [152].

In Vietnamese trade association assembly halls and temples, as in other parts of Southeast Asia where there were settlements of Chinese immigrants, the structure and arrangement of the spaces as well as the decorative features owe their form to Chinese models. Roof decorations made of *jian nian*, ceramic tile pieces arranged in a colourful mosaic to depict auspicious animals and other motifs, were peculiar to the immigrant Chinese communities, the ceramic pieces usually imported from Chinese factories [153].

Another strand of Chinese thought that influenced artistic conceptions in Vietnam was Mahayana Buddhism, in which bodhisattvas, or saints, played a major part. Of particular

153 Depiction of a *qilin* constructed of ceramic shards, *jian nian*, outside a pagoda in Nha Trang, Vietnam. The *qilin*, a creature with scales and hooves and sometimes a single horn, is a traditional Chinese symbol of longevity and happiness.

importance was Avalokiteshvara, in China reinterpreted as the Goddess of Mercy Kuan Yin, known in Vietnam as Quan Am [155]. As the personification of divine assistance and compassion, particularly toward the childless, her statue appears in countless manifestations and has come to dominate Buddhist imagery in Vietnam. Statues of the Buddha himself also show the influence of Chinese interpretation, though the emphasis on wooden carving and sculpture has more in common with styles found in other parts of Southeast Asia than it does with Chinese traditions. Buddhist architecture also contains echoes of Chinese forms. The Linh Mu pagoda just outside Hue, founded in the seventeenth century, is dominated by the seven-storey Tower of Happiness and Grace added in the mid-nineteenth century, which is reminiscent of older Chinese multi-tiered pagodas [154]. On each floor is an altar to a different Buddha.

Elements of Buddhist iconography are as prevalent in Vietnam as they are in other Southeast Asian art traditions, but their use is less allusive and more ornamental. The eight Buddhist symbols,

154 The Phuoc Duyen tower at the Linh Mu pagoda near Hue, built by the Nguyen emperor Thieu Tri in 1844.

Indian in origin, under Chinese influence become almost formulaic. The lotus, wheel, vase, conch shell, endless knot, twin fish, royal canopy and state umbrellas are still ubiquitous, but in contemporary Vietnam such symbols are more likely to be seen as referring to good fortune than to specifically Buddhist ideas.

Taoist conceptions of the universe also found their way to Vietnam. Central to them is the balanced opposition of yin and yang, represented from the Tang dynasty onward at the centre of the eight 'trigrams', symbols of the basic elements and directions of the cosmos. In addition the figures of the eight Taoist immortals, identified by the attributes they carry, provided the subject matter for much Vietnamese art, though their stories are largely forgotten. Also widely depicted are the three originally Chinese figures known in Vietnam as Phuc, Loc, and Tho, representing respectively prosperity, happiness and long life, again identifiable by iconographic attributes [156]. The desire for

155 Quan Am, the Vietnamese Goddess of Mercy, plays a central role in Mahayana Buddhism in Vietnam. Here she appears as Avalokiteshvara, with a thousand eyes and arms. Ninh Phuc Temple, But Thap, Bac Ninh, Vietnam. 17th century.

longevity is core to Taoist ideas, and has affected the art of Vietnam in two ways. One is the prevalence of talismanic motifs designed to repel disease and misfortune and thus prevent an early death. Another is through symbols referring specifically to long life, including stone carvings of the tortoise, on whose back stelae are carried in memorial structures both in China and in Vietnam, carved with inscriptions recounting the lives of those whom they commemorate.

While Chinese influence can be seen throughout the art of the Vietnamese, in other parts of the region this was largely confined to areas where communities of immigrant Chinese settled. Among those Chinese who were attracted to the Malay Peninsula after the establishment of the British Straits Settlements in the early nineteenth century, a hybrid culture emerged in which the men retained elements of Chinese culture such as the veneration of ancestors, clan affiliation and trade guilds, while the women, though influenced by ideas and practices from China, mixed with them Malay customs and materials. The most visible aspect of Chinese influence was in architecture, which was dominated by Chinese ideology and ornamentation. Houses of the well-to-do in Straits Chinese communities were governed by the rules of feng shui, with an airwell in the centre to allow air to circulate. Facing the main entrance in the front hall was the household altar dedicated to the guardian deity of the family. The altar was traditionally made of Chinese blackwood, though teak might

156 The eight Taoist immortals are depicted on the upper panel of this embroidered altar cloth, or *tok wie*. The six men and two women gained immortality by following Taoist principles, each having colourful adventures on their journey. They appear frequently in Chinese art in the region, each identifiable by various attributes. The three figures below personify longevity, prosperity and happiness. Georgetown, Penang, Malaysia.

157 Ancestral altar in the Chan House, Malacca, now the Baba Nyonya Heritage Museum. Note the elaborately carved furniture, incense containers and the *tok wie*, or altar cloth, at the front.

sometimes be substituted. Behind the front entrance hall was the hall of the ancestors, with another altar housing the ancestral shrine [157]. Here, unlike their Chinese equivalents, where an image of the patriarch would be displayed, Straits households usually displayed an image of the matriarch. The accoutrements surrounding the images of the figures on both altars were often imported from China.

This hybrid culture that grew up in the Straits Settlements had its roots in earlier times. Prior to the introduction of steam-powered shipping, many Chinese traders in maritime Southeast Asia had been obliged by the direction of the trade winds to spend a considerable part of the year in the region, and of these, many married locally. Among groups such as the Malays, whose sense of family included those related both by descent and by marriage, this would entail living in the wife's family home, a phenomenon at odds with the strongly patrilineal Chinese way of life. Many Chinese abandoned the culture of their homeland, taking up the Malay language, cultural practices and artistic styles. Nevertheless, motifs and ideas from China were often introduced into the Malay artistic vocabulary through this route. Symbols of good fortune, prosperity and happiness and other iconographic elements were incorporated into items associated with rites of passage such as marriage. Thus the batik produced on the north coast of Java may include auspicious symbols such as the dragon (for a boy) or the phoenix (for a girl). The butterfly is specifically a symbol of wedded bliss, the peony of prosperity, the upright bamboo of righteousness and the qilin, or unicorn, of wisdom, justice and success. The swastika, a symbol that originally derives from a pun on the Chinese word for 'ten thousand' and meaning by extension abundance and fecundity, often appears as a background filling motif [158]. Most of these symbols derived from Chinese folklore have in Southeast Asia come to signify good fortune in general, and the particular logic and significance of each one has been largely forgotten. But they live on in the fish, dog-lions, bats and chrysanthemums scattered over the colourful designs of sarongs, shoulder cloths and slings for carrying babies. These emblems appear not just in the work of Chinese communities, but in neighbouring groups who have adopted and reinterpreted them in their own work.

The colours employed in batik on the north coast of Java in the first half of the twentieth century were also more in line with Chinese taste than those found further inland, favouring bright pastels over the sombre brown and dark blue of classic court

styles still adhered to in central Java. A similar preference for
greens, yellows and pinks characterized the ceramics favoured by
the Straits Chinese [159]. This Nyonyaware, as it came to be
known, was said to be manufactured at Jingdezhen in Jianxi
province, where the Chinese imperial porcelain factory was
based, though it is more likely to have originated in Dehua near
Amoy in Fujian. The multicoloured decoration that covered the
surface of the white body employed the auspicious motifs of
Chinese tradition, as with batik, though the style was very much
designed to suit the preferences of the Chinese of Southeast Asia.

Chinese Southeast Asians did create some of their own
decorative art. While many of the trappings of the wedding
ceremony were imported from China, well-to-do brides were
expected to embroider items in their trousseaux. The stitches
they employed were derived from the homeland: satin stitch for
flat areas of colour and the Peking knot where a denser texture or
richer blend of colour was needed. Fine beadwork was another
accomplishment of the women of the community, often used to
embellish the slippers of bride and groom. Silverware, gold and
jewelry were sometimes commissioned from other ethnic groups
[160]: some households had their designs made up by Singhalese
jewellers, for example. Silverwork from Thailand and Indonesia

158 Detail of a batik shawl,
selendang, with a filling motif, or
isen, consisting of the swastika, or
banji, design. Indramayu, West Java.

175

159 Ceramic *kamcheng*, a covered jar with supports at each side, which would normally hold brass ring handles. The lid is topped by a dog-lion finial. The standing phoenix and peony in the ogival panel are typical of Nyonyaware, or Straits Chinese porcelain.

was commonly used by the Chinese community. But there were also Chinese gold- and silversmiths working in Southeast Asia, and they quickly took up the styles of local craftsmen. Southeast Asian techniques and styles differ somewhat from those of the Chinese mainland, with embossing, granulation and repoussé the dominant methods employed. The elaborate embellishment of Southeast Asian silverware, its surfaces filled with curling foliate and vegetal forms, narrative scenes or auspicious emblems such as the signs of the zodiac, contrasted with the smooth surfaces favoured in China, where the decoration was more often chased into the surface.

The degree of Chinese influence in Southeast Asia has thus varied widely from time to time and from place to place. Among the elite of Vietnam, Chinese aesthetic models held sway for many centuries into independence, right through to the twentieth century. Iconographic references to the dragon, phoenix, unicorn and lotus were widespread and continued to feature especially in the applied arts of Vietnam. At lower levels of society, however, indigenous traditions persisted after the rejection of Chinese rule, flourishing outside the urban centres for many centuries. In other parts of the region, Chinese influence has been more piecemeal, and nowhere has it dominated artistic forms. Despite the widespread appearance of motifs, materials and techniques derived from China, these were rarely adopted without alteration and Chinese artistic forms were gradually softened and overlain by other influences over succeeding centuries. Nevertheless, artists throughout the region have drawn inspiration from Chinese ideas in their work.

160 Nyonya brides traditionally carried ceremonial handkerchiefs, sometimes made of silver. In this example, auspicious symbols from both Chinese and Hindu-Buddhist cultural worlds are worked in repoussé. The bat at the apex, the pheasant, the lotus and the vase of plenty all carry explicit meanings. 405 × 137 mm.

Chapter 7   Modern times

For the most part, ideas from Europe had very little impact on artistic expression in Southeast Asia in the years following the arrival of the first Europeans in the sixteenth century. However, by the time colonial domination began its decline in the early twentieth century, new forces had begun to appear in the art of the region. The upsurge in resistance to the colonial presence was accompanied by nationalist movements which worked through a range of channels, including the arts. At the same time the royal courts, which had been the major sponsors of many forms of art, largely lost their central role as patrons. Art institutions which had been founded during or in the wake of European dominance gave rise to a new kind of creative work. In most cases, this meant that artists drew on imagery and media from their pasts, especially from the periods when their nation had held sway over a considerable area. In Cambodia, it was the Angkorean empire that provided the source of inspiration; in Thailand it was the art of Sukhothai. Parallel experiences of political and social change in the various newly emerging nations led to similar developments in their art, albeit in a complex melding of forms, media and ideas. However, western notions of art also played some part in shaping the new movements that came into existence in the early twentieth century, as initially did Chinese practices and perceptions, particularly in Thailand and in the areas that were eventually to form the nation states of Singapore, Malaysia and Indonesia.

In the aftermath of the Second World War, Indonesia, the Philippines and Burma gained their independence, followed not long after by Malaya and Singapore, Cambodia and Laos. The situation in Vietnam was more complicated, with the division of the country in 1954 into two parts. This was followed by continuing conflict, prolonged by American involvement and also affecting Vietnam's neighbours, Cambodia and Laos. In the latter

161 Panya Vijintanasarn et al., *The Defeat of Mara and the Enlightenment*, 1984–87. Acrylic and spray paint. Mural at the Buddhapadipa temple, Wimbledon, UK.

162 Amongst Balinese artists it is the painters of Kamasan, a traditional centre of court painting, who have been most concerned to preserve traditional narrative styles. 1505 × 876 mm.

two countries and in Burma, internal instability meant that little attention was given to the concerns of artists during this time.

One of the places where western art had most impact in the early years of the twentieth century was the Indonesian island of Bali, where a group of western artists formed an enclave whose influence on local production was considerable and far-reaching. The most well-known of these artists were the German Walter Spies and the Dutchman Rudolf Bonnet, who encouraged Balinese painters to depict scenes from daily life in their work. Previously, the stories from the Ramayana and Mahabharata had provided the chief subject matter for paintings on cloth, or *ider-ider*, which were hung along the eaves of buildings during religious

ceremonies, or for murals such as those at the court of justice at Klungkung [162]. Alongside changes in subject matter came a change in materials and forms, with the introduction of machine-woven cloth to replace the handwoven cotton used before. Paintings were smaller and more portable, and the traditional colours, many once made from earth pigments, soot or bones, were superseded by acrylic paints. In the past paintings had been largely composed of human and divine figures painted in profile, like the figures of shadow puppetry, but now new styles began to emerge.

In 1936 Bonnet and Spies helped a local prince in Ubud to set up a painters' cooperative, Pita Maha, which organized exhibitions of paintings to be sold on the art market. It was the two Europeans who were largely responsible for selecting those works deemed to be of sufficient quality for exhibition. Thus western taste, mediated both by the purchasers and by Spies and Bonnet, began to play a part in determining the style of Balinese art. The painters, used to an apprentice system whereby they were trained to emulate a master, often responded to the Europeans' comments by copying their approach. Other centres in Bali developed styles of their own. In the village of Batuan the work was darker, and the subjects remained mythological for the most part [163, 164]. In the village of Kerambitan, traditional wayang figures were retained though they were more boldly delineated than in the past and the palette was wider.

In the late 1950s, another Balinese school developed at Penestanan, where the Dutch artist Arie Smit encouraged local boys to paint in a naïve style which became popular with tourists and western collectors, both of which groups were increasingly important consumers of the new art. Around 1940, Balinese sculptors adopted a distinct style for their wood carvings, dominated by smooth, elongated figures. Some individual painters used painting to explore their inner states – using surreal elements to express spiritual and psychological ideas. The work of these and other painters was increasingly sought after, as the notion of art as individual expression took hold.

Elsewhere in Indonesia, the earliest artist to be affected by western influence was Raden Saleh, a nineteenth-century Javanese aristocrat who lived and painted in Europe for more than twenty years, and who mastered the conventional techniques and styles of the day. No-one followed this approach until the 1920s, however, and those who did were quickly challenged by a group of artists led by Soedjojono, who in the following decade urged the need for art in Indonesia to reflect the aspirations of the nation in its drive toward independence. Not until this had been achieved, however, did artists find a new voice in their work, the only exception being the renowned painter Affandi, who had drawn on Expressionism but developed his own distinctly Indonesian idiom.

As the twentieth century progressed there was a gradual and increasing rejection of western ideas. In Indonesia this took place in the aftermath of the rejection of Dutch rule, the struggle against Japanese occupation and then the final push in the mid 1940s to achieve independence. There was a brief but intense time known as the 'Sanggar period' (1945–49) when the focus in art was either on the political struggles that dominated the early years of

163 & 164 Two scenes from a tale in which a young woman is abducted by a naga. 163 preparations for a wedding feast. 164 on the left a couple carry the head of the *naga* in an underwater scene, and on the right they present it to an elder. Ink on paper, Batuan, Bali. *c.* 1938. Both 266.7 × 228.6 mm.

independence, or on formal explorations of aesthetics. After that, artists drew heavily on traditional imagery and subject matter in a search for an Indonesian style. Motifs that permeated traditional art, such as the mountain and the ship, and depictions of traditional performance arts such as Balinese and Javanese dance, could evoke a sense of nationhood for the majority of the population and were frequently used as thematic emblems. Aspects of Javanese culture in particular were adopted as national symbols. Images taken from the sculptures of Borobudur and Prambanan, or even images of the temples themselves, were widely incorporated into art intended to speak to the nation as a whole [166]. Similarly, the distinctive profiles of the wayang kulit shadow puppets frequently appeared as elements in artistic composition, and batik, once regarded as an exclusively Javanese preserve, was used as a medium by many artists. Balinese artists who trained in Java retained a Balinese identity for their work by incorporating subject matter expressing their origin: landscapes, scenes of Balinese dance and cili figures, for example. The most notable exponent of genre painting was Hendra Gunawan [165], who led the People's Painters in the late 1940s and 1950s. After the fall of Soekharno in 1965 this type of subject matter was seen as subversive and discouraged.

The establishment of two new institutions in 1950, an art department at the Bandung Institute of Technology and the

165 Hendra Gunawan's depictions of the lives of ordinary Indonesians were at one time condemned as communist propaganda. He is widely regarded as one of Indonesia's greatest artists. *Nursing the Neighbour's Baby*, 1975. Oil on canvas. 940 × 1490 mm.

166 Srihadi Sudarso, *Borobudur*,
1982. Oil on canvas, 1000 ×
1400 mm.

national Art Academy in Yogyakarta, led to a new era in the
nation's art. The emphasis now was on individual expression, with
students being encouraged to take their place in the international
art world through studying the history of both Asian and
European art. Their work was to be recognizably part of the
broad oeuvre of modern art, while at the same time imbued with
an Indonesian character. This was achieved largely through
incorporating some traditional elements, whether in terms of
subject matter, technique or materials. Continuing this approach,
many Indonesian artists have in recent years embraced installation
and performance art [167].

In Thailand by the early twentieth century there was already
considerable interest in the art of the western world. King
Mongkut, who reigned from 1851 to 1868, had encouraged
European diplomats and technical advisers at his court, and the
influence of western styles is evident in much of the architecture,
which he sponsored. Palaces, temples and many administrative
buildings combine styles and decorative features of Thai, western

and Chinese traditions. In a number of temple murals, including those painted on the walls surrounding the Temple of the Emerald Buddha, three-dimensional perspective was introduced, though the subjects remained depictions of traditional Thai scenes. In Khrua In Khong's murals at Wat Bowon Nivet in Bangkok, European ships and Thai people in western apparel were painted in a style owing much to western models [168].

King Mongkut's son, King Chulalongkorn, continued his father's forward-looking perspective and visited Europe twice. He brought back not just ideas for technical and economic advancement, but also architects, painters and sculptors, mostly from Italy. These artists worked together with their Thai counterparts at court, so that the way art was regarded and the forms that it took in Thailand underwent gradual transformation. One of the most far-reaching changes was a greater concern with realism and the techniques by which it might be achieved.

King Chulalongkorn's son and successor, King Vajiravudh, retained his father's interest in art but felt that a revival of traditional Thai approaches was needed to restore vitality to the county's artistic expression. In 1912 he established the Department of Fine Arts and the following year the Arts and Crafts School, where instruction was provided in a range of visual and performance arts. Nevertheless Vajiravudh commissioned a number of overseas artists to work on the decoration of various palaces and throne halls. He also commissioned paintings

167 Heri Dono is probably best known for his collage and acrylic works from the 1990s depicting wild and gaudy distorted figures, at the same time humorous and frightening. His exploration of *wayang* and other village performances have inspired much of his installation and performance work. Heri Dono, *Wild Horse*, performed in Yogyakarta, 1992.

commemorating events in his father's reign and statues and monuments for the Royal Palace. The Italian sculptor Corrado Feroci was responsible for many of these, and it was court patronage of this particular artist that had the most influence on the development of modern Thai art. For the decades following his arrival in Thailand in 1923 until his death in 1962, Feroci (or Silpa Bhirasri, the name he adopted for himself) acted as a father figure and mentor for generations of Thai artists.

In previous centuries, young Thai artists had traditionally served an apprenticeship under a master painter or sculptor, who would set them exercises in technique which trained them in every aspect of their work. There had been relatively little room for variation in style or content, and the concept of art as the expression of an individual vision was completely unknown. Silpa Bhirasri's position was paradoxically both to encourage artists to develop their own skills and styles and thus break free from the constraints of their predecessors, and to serve as the master whose lead was followed by his disciples. In particular, he

169 Hien Yimsiri, *Musical Rhythm*, 1949. Cast metal. Height 540 mm.

170 Fua Haribhitak, *Composition*, 1955. 880 × 650 mm.

171 Prasong Padamanya, *Wat Pho*, 1958. Poster colours. 870 × 1070 mm.

encouraged Thai painters to study in the European tradition, painting in oils and following western conventions of drawing and portraiture and, most importantly, sculpture.

Bhirasri persuaded the Thai government to establish a university of the arts, now Silpakorn University. There he inspired his students to look for new ways of expressing their visions of the Thai world. The curriculum included the techniques and history of both Thai classical art and that of Europe. For a long time, Thai artists produced work in the European idiom, and for the most part of European subjects. They explored and echoed the work of Impressionists, Cubists, Surrealists and Post-Impressionists. One of Bhirasri's pupils who had a great influence on the next generation was Fua Haribhitak, whose work was in many ways indistinguishable from that of a European artist, albeit in a style which had been superseded in Europe by several decades [170].

For most of the first half of the twentieth century, artists in Thailand continued to work largely in western genres such as still life and portraiture, their subjects including non-traditional figures such as ballet dancers, piano players and nudes. Nevertheless, the distinctly Thai vision underlying this work was beginning to become evident, in the elegant positioning of the body and

modelling of the fingers of Khien Yimsiri's *Musical Rhythm* (1949), for example [169], or the repeating shapes of the chedi spires in Prasong Padamanuja's *Wat Pho* (1958) [171].

The revived interest in Thailand's artistic past can be traced to a number of phenomena. One was the establishment in the late 1970s of a department of traditional classical Thai art at Silpakorn University. Here, students were encouraged to explore and re-articulate traditional Thai art forms, from both folk and classical traditions. At the same time most artists who had achieved any prominence had undertaken some training overseas, especially in America and Britain, and this led to a more confident command of and experimentation with newer western forms. These two developments fused together, so that many Thai artists embraced both the old and the new, the western and the eastern, to create art that was recognizably Thai in essence. Thus while art continued its traditional role in Thai society, as an expression of devotion both to religious belief and to the king, the influence of the west was not rejected in the way that it was in other Southeast Asian countries. In a country that had fought no battles to obtain independence from colonial powers, there was perhaps less need for art to express a national identity. More widespread was the desire to engage with international art movements, accompanied by a rise in awareness of the effects of capitalism, urbanization and globalization as threats to Thai values and ways of life. Since the 1960s, many Thai artists have made such concerns explicit in their work.

Art academies still dominate Thai art. The work of their contemporary artists tends to be well crafted, and the skill of the artist in controlling his or her materials is always evident.

172 Montien Boonma, *Water*, 1991. Soil pigment on *saa* paper, terracotta jars with smoke and soil pigment. 3800 × 4500 × 400 mm.

Traditionally, Thailand has judged art primarily in terms of fineness of line and detail and intricacy of composition. Together with the rigorous training in technique which Thai art institutions provide, this means that works can often be appreciated in terms of their craftsmanship in addition to their expressive qualities. Thai artists tend also to be serious and thoughtful, most intending their work to communicate a discernible meaning to their audiences. Many find their subject matter in inner spiritual or religious worlds. Montien Boonma's work, for example, is imbued with Buddhist ideals, which extend to his choice of his materials, recycled natural elements which echo the Buddhist precept that everything is inherently changeable [172]. His art is intensely introspective, spiritual and religious, and the sincerity of his work has been an essential component in defining his status as a respected Thai artist. Panya Vijintanasarn's work is also characterized by its concern with Buddhism. Between 1985 and 1987 he painted the murals of the Buddhapadipa Temple in Wimbledon, England, including in the paintings figures and ideas that make reference to events and developments in society not traditional subjects for depiction on temple walls, showing that religion and individuals must engage with contemporary issues [161]. There are many other artists whose work is still more outward-looking and who tackle social, political and environmental subjects in their work. Sutee Kunavichyanant is concerned with the need for people to sustain those aspects of the world they value if these are not to become empty and die. *White Elephant* (1999) consists of a life-sized elephant figure lying on its side, with hoses attached extending to the viewers, who must pedal air into it to keep it inflated [173]. Most recently, artists have begun to comment on the role and form of art itself.

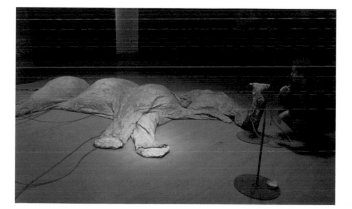

173 Sutee Kunavichyanant, *White Elephant*, 1999.

Until 1925, art in Vietnam was largely created in the service of the pagoda, temple or village community. In that year the French colonial government set up an 'Ecole Supérieure des Beaux-Arts' in Hanoi. As part of the education system administered by the French, it was modelled on its counterparts in France, and its curriculum and approach were largely the same. Its attitude to art was deeply conservative, following the precepts of the French Academy and largely ignoring the more revolutionary ideas being promulgated about art in Europe at that time. There was some attention given to oriental art forms, however, and after a while there were concessions to Vietnamese traditions, with the introduction of lacquerwork and silk painting to the repertoire.

Nonetheless training was largely geared toward classical western genres and styles: nude studies, street scenes and portraiture were the dominant forms. A command of technique rather than an exploration of new ideas was clearly the aim of both the students and their teachers. There is little evidence of a challenge to the existing order, political or artistic, in works from the period leading up to the Second World War. A few artists, notably Nguyen Gia Tri, Nguyen Tuong Lan, To Ngoc Van and Tran Van Can, stand out as the founding figures of modern Vietnamese art, largely because of their mastery of the new techniques they

174 Nguyen Gia Tri, *Women*, 1951–56. Lacquer. 510 × 720 mm.

learnt and also their role as teachers, giving confidence to the next generation [174].

The 1945 revolution led to the founding of a democratic republic in the north of Vietnam. The war that followed, beginning in December 1946, set the French against the Communist-led Vietnamese government, and was echoed by a split in artistic allegiances. The Communist line was that patriotic art should serve the nation and the people rather than the interests of imperialism and the bourgeoisie. Cubism, Impressionism and other modernist movements were denounced as decadent and opportunistic. Some artists, such as Nguyen Gia Tri and Ta Ty, had been heavily influenced by these schools, and found it hard to break away. Others were happier to see the function of their work as the promotion of the revolution, and while they retained the materials and media of the west, they abandoned its stylistic approaches. With French rule restored in parts of the north, some of the teachers of the old Ecole began in 1950 to teach in the newly formed underground Ecole des Beaux-Arts, which was to become the foundation of Vietnamese modern art. Socialist Realism was the style they taught, and the subject matter became the key element in any work. Artworks were to depict workers,

175 Tran Van Can, *Militia Women in the Coastal Zone*, 1960. Oil. 600 × 820 mm.

peasants and soldiers, expressing their outlook and reflecting the reality of their lives [175]. Qualitative judgments about art were based on the responses of ordinary people rather than those of elite critics trained in western aesthetic modes of appreciation. This new articulation of the role of art and its relationship to society meant that Vietnamese art took on and expressed explicit meaning.

Four artists began to dominate the Vietnamese art scene: Nguyen Sang, the designer of the bank notes for the new republic, Xuan Phai, Nguyen Tu Nghiem and Duong Bich Lien. Art reflected official ideology, contributing to campaigns for literacy, land reform and industrialization. Much of this work was centred around a new official Ecole des Beaux-Arts, founded in Hanoi in 1955, where art was defined in terms of its contribution to social solidarity. Throughout the war with the United States, from 1965 to 1973, artists remained heavily engaged in patriotic work, producing propaganda posters which celebrated the heroism of those who took part in the struggle. Thus, although Vietnamese art rejected western forms, it was heavily influenced by models from contemporary China and more particularly the Soviet Union, and there was less of an attempt than there had been in other countries in the region to seek a truly national identity. Some work did follow this route, however, using silk and lacquer as media, for example, or Vietnamese calligraphy as key motifs.

After the American defeat in 1973, the narrow strictures that had governed artistic styles since the founding of the democratic republic loosened to some extent. In the south, a more eclectic vision of art allowing artists to experiment and to explore their own individuality had continued to flourish. After reunification in 1976 artists throughout Vietnam felt more free to explore abstract elements of form, colour and line and to move away from representational art [176]. Today, art in Vietnam is characterized by bold experimentation and vibrancy, which reflects a growing sense of confidence in the country.

In the part of Southeast Asia that experienced British rule, later to become Malaysia, the indigenous inhabitants had little to do with western art. In the nineteenth century Malays underwent an Islamic revival that militated against acceptance of the representational artistic forms favoured by colonial artists. Few Malays had a western-style education, and those who did attend English-language schools generally concentrated their efforts on subjects more likely to improve their economic and social position.

Thus it was not until the early twentieth century that some of those educated in English- and Chinese-speaking schools began to take an interest in western ideas about art. Those living in urban centres such as Georgetown (Penang), Malacca, Kuala Lumpur and Singapore, which had long been relatively cosmopolitan in outlook, were the first to do so. Early forays into the field took the form of figurative work based on observation rather than the more symbolic and religious traditions of indigenous art. The new approach allowed artists from a range of ethnic backgrounds to come together through a focus on individualistic notions of self-expression rather than a continuity of form and style. Landscape, portraiture and still life were established in media that were also new to this part of the world, such as oil and watercolour painting.

The most influential institution in the years following the Second World War was the Nanyang Academy of Fine Arts based

176 Bui Xuan Phai, *Cheo* 1987. Poster colours. 210 × 160 mm.

177 Syed Ahmad Jamal, *The Bait*,
1959. Oil on board. 1540 mm ×
1220 mm.

in Singapore. Many of the teachers had come there from mainland China, where Socialist Realism had been introduced in the years following the 1911 revolution. But Chinese artists at that time had also studied the work of members of the Impressionist, Cubist and Fauvist schools. To their pupils they imparted a sense of themselves as individuals searching for their own artistic language, free from the constraints of the past. They experimented with form and technique, leaving behind conventional media and iconography, though their work was still informed by elements from the Far East.

By the 1950s some local artists had studied at art institutions in Europe and developed in their work ideas of abstract art derived from Cubism and Expressionism. The freedom to express their experience of the world was appealing. However, they did not slavishly follow the west, and they continued to refer to the Asian context. In Syed Ahmad Jamal's *The Bait*, the swirling forms on a white background evoke both the free brushwork of Chinese painting and the elegance of calligraphic forms [177]. Abstract

178 Yeoh Jin Leng, *Padi Field, Orchard, Hill, Sky*, 1963. Oil on canvas. 830 × 1020 mm.

Expressionism was used as a vehicle through which western and Asian styles could become fused.

During the colonial period, artists in Malaysia rarely used art as a medium for exploring social and political issues. Nevertheless, some did express aspects of the colonial condition in their work. In particular, some Chinese-educated artists belonging to the 'Equator Group', which was associated with the Communist uprising in British Malaya in the late 1940s and early 1950s, adopted the Socialist Realist style, depicting, for example, conditions of labour amongst the poor. The 'Equator Group' was banned by the British and later, after independence, by the Singapore government. A few later artists of the Nanyang group portrayed social conditions, but most paintings of people during this period were romanticized and pastoral; even those in realist mode were not directed at changing attitudes or conditions in a way which was socially engaged.

Gaining independence in 1957 had a considerable effect on the Malaysian art world. The ruling United Malay National

Organization (UMNO) agitated for a Malay-centred nationalism. The Malay landscape became a central image; fertile rice fields were a recurrent metaphor for the emerging young nation, along with idealistic images of tranquil people [178]. Following on from this came the inclusion of elements from the past that could contribute to a national cultural identity.

In 1969 there were riots arising from ethnic tensions between those who regarded themselves as indigenous and those descended from more recent immigrant groups, especially the Chinese. Two years later the National Cultural Congress gave official sanction to Malay cultural values and forms over those of other ethnic groups, and this became the centre of National Cultural Policy, though other indigenous groups were also given privileges.

The new cultural policy gave encouragement to the inclusion of Islamic references and motifs, and methods derived from Malay artistic traditions such as woodcarving, jewelry, gold thread embroidery and other decorative arts. In 1978 an exhibition of traditional Malay applied art at the University of Malaya helped to strengthen Malay identity and pride, and gave particular impetus to artists training at the Mara Institute of Technology's School of Art and Design. During this period, myths and legends from Malay literature frequently served as the focus of subject matter. In the 1980s these developments became part of the wider international Islamic revivalist movement, with a consequent emphasis on ornate, non-representational surface decoration [180].

The greater social and political consciousness that emerged among non-Malay artists following the National Cultural Congress of 1971 led many to question their own positions and the focus of their work. Some artists from Chinese ethnic backgrounds brought elements of Chinese culture and ideology into their work, using ideograms and symbols from Chinese folk art as visual motifs. Others produced more figurative pictorial representations of Chinese subjects, highlighting the Chinese presence in the Malaysian community, Chinese festivals and the cultural distance between young and older generations of Chinese Malaysians. Artists of Indian descent have similarly explored the social position of Indian minorities in Malaysia through themes such as religious festivals and other Indian cultural manifestations.

The work of artists such as Kelvin Chap Lok Leong has highlighted other sections of Malaysia's polyglot population: images of people from the Iban indigenous minority and other groups jostle for position in his work [179]. The simple frame on

179 Kelvin Chap Kok Leong,
Belawing, Keramen, Mamat, 1995.
Mixed media. 1410 × 570 × 510 mm.

which his work *Belawing, Keramen, Mamat* is stretched evokes the forest context beyond the normal sphere of Malay life.

An expanding vision of Malaysia as part of a greater Asian region informs much of the more recent work of Malaysian artists. Many have started to look beyond ethnic issues to problems of global capitalism, pollution and the degradation of the forest environment. Artists now employ a whole range of media, from three-dimensional constructed forms made of a multiplicity of

180 Both an aerial perspective and also the sense that the spectator is looking up, gaining a glimpse of the heavens, are suggested here. The field is divided by successively smaller superimposed frames, filled with surface patterning. Mastura Abdul Rahman, *Interior no. 29*, 1987. Mixed media. 1120 × 1155 mm.

natural and synthetic materials to installation art incorporating video and computer technology.

The situation in the Philippines differed from that in other Southeast Asian countries, in that European influence on art began much earlier. The Spanish colonizers had also made greater attempts, and had more success in converting the local population to Christianity. The impact of their evangelizing mission penetrated deeper and was more widespread than that of the Dutch in Indonesia, the British in Malaysia and the French in Indo-China, though each of these had presided over the conversion of a proportion of those populations. During the Spanish colonial period, which lasted from 1565 until 1898, local artists were introduced to the styles and techniques employed in western religious art, in particular Catholic iconography as represented in prayer books and other religious literature. Philippine arts had always been associated with religion, so the impact of widespread conversion to Christianity on art was profound.

By the early nineteenth century, economic changes were also

181 Victorio Edades, *The Builders*, 1928. Oil on board.

182 Fernando Amorsolo, *Rice Fields*, 1952. Oil on canvas laid down on board. 600 × 850 mm.

encouraging artistic change. The creation of a wealthier class of merchants and landlords resulting from the introduction of cash crops and the development of international trade led to a new market for art. The emerging bourgeoisie began to commission secular works of art and architecture to express their cultural refinement and superior status. Portraits became fashionable, as evidence of the prosperity of their patrons.

In the Philippines, as elsewhere in the region, a few local artists had the opportunity to study overseas. Foremost amongst these were Juan Luna and Felix Resurreccion Hidalgo, who for the most part followed the conventions established by the art academies of Europe. An essential part of their repertoire was the depiction of classical subjects in the style of ancient Greece or Rome. Such work had little resonance for those who came after them, however.

Unlike this change in other parts of the region, the introduction of local subject matter here did not accompany a desire to assert a Philippine national identity. As in Bali, the demand for local landscapes and scenes of peasant life was fuelled by the expatriate community. Under the American regime, from 1901 until 1941, officials, tourists and merchants encouraged the production of paintings of idyllic genre subjects. The most famous exponent of this type of art was Fernando Amorsolo, working in the early twentieth century [182].

Some Philippine artists had begun in the early twentieth century to use their work to challenge the role of the church and the colonial regime. The works of artists such as Jose Pereyra and Jorge Pineda, which appeared in publications of the time, gave art a new agenda. A further development took place with the arrival of Modernism, espoused and promoted by Victorio Edades, widely regarded as the 'Father of Modernism' in the Philippines [181]. By this time, the art establishment in the Philippines was firmly in the hands of those trained in the academic conventions, and the modern approach to art as a medium of self-expression, within which each artist sought his own voice, was staunchly resisted by the institutions. Nevertheless, a number of groups emerged to challenge the old order, and by the mid 1950s, Modernism had taken its place at the centre of the Philippine art stage.

In the second half of the twentieth century, a variety of routes was taken by Philippine artists. One was to explore Abstract Expressionism, though the results tended to be derivative of French and American models, with artists struggling to find a national voice. Earlier in the century, some artists had espoused

183 Manuel 'Boy' Rodrigues Jnr., *Tinggians*, 1978. Painted and dyed cloth on plywood. 1540 × 1290 mm.

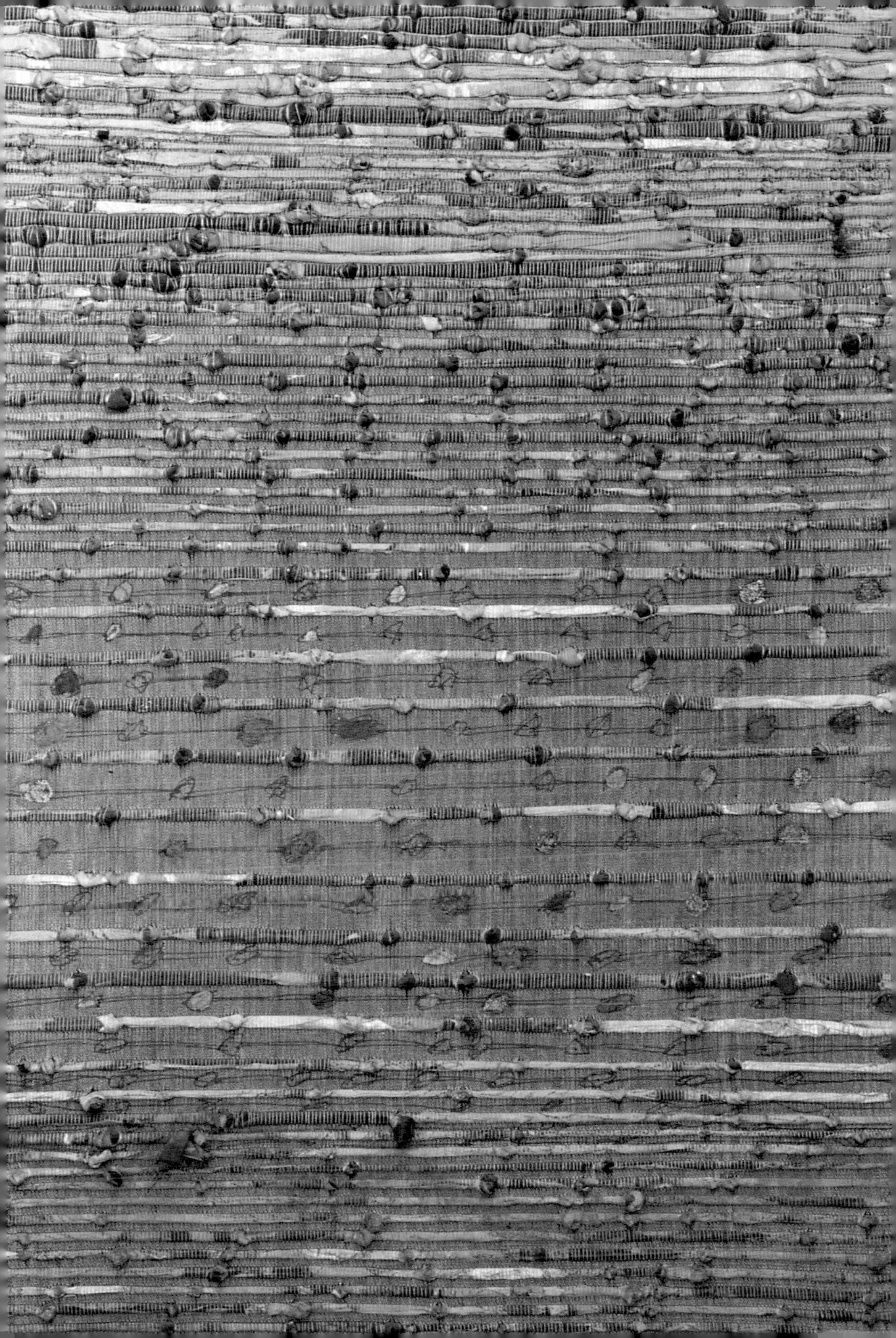

neo-realism, exploring social themes and documenting the lives of the poor. Later artists depicted the same subjects but with less of a social agenda, rather as an expression of Philippine identity. Representational styles of art continued among landscape artists and by those exploring magic realism. In the late 1960s figurative art took on a political dimension as artists became concerned to respond to current issues. More recently, artists have been more experimental in their use of materials, and three-dimensional art has become more widespread [183]. As elsewhere in Southeast Asia, as the Philippines have become more confident in their identity and their autonomy, artists have become less preoccupied with finding a national style and their work has taken its place in the context of an international art world.

Southeast Asian art has always been characterized by a strong tradition of continuity, and in many parts of the region artistic works continue to reflect forms and underlying conceptions of the world that have remained if not static then at least stable for centuries. Where there have been changes in belief, for example where Christianity has become the dominant religion, the iconography of the new faith has generally been subsumed into a pre-existing aesthetic, merging with indigenous forms expressing earlier beliefs. Outside the academies and the international art market, work in traditional media is still produced. However, economic, social and environmental changes are having an increasing effect, both on the nature of the art produced and on the motivation of those who produce it. In the face of increasing pressures such as industrialization, urbanization and tourism, the whole context of such traditional production has been transformed. Only time will tell what impact these changes will have on the work of future generations of Southeast Asian artists.

Glossary

adu zatua ancestor figures from Nias, used by the living to communicate with the dead.

Angkor capital city of the Khmer empire in the late 9th and early 10th centuries and from the 11th to 14th centuries

Angkor Thom royal city rebuilt at Angkor around 1200

Angkor Wat temple built by Suryavarman II in the first half of the 12th century

Annam name used by Europeans to refer to the area in what is now central Vietnam where a French protectorate was established in 1885

Arjuna Wiwaha poem written in Old Javanese about the wedding of Arjuna, one of the heroes of the Mahabharata

Asoka (c. 304–232 BC) ruler of an empire covering much of India, who adopted Buddhism and became its patron

asura type of demon

Avalokiteshvara (Sanskrit) one of the five main bodhisattvas of Mahayana Buddhism, the personification of compassion

Ayutthaya kingdom established in 1350, with its capital on the Lopburi river in the lower reaches of the Chao Phrya valley

balai (Indonesian) open pavilion, sometimes used as meeting house

Bangkok period from 1782 to the present, also known as Ratanakosin period, during which the Thai capital has been Bangkok

batik technique of decorating textiles by applying wax to resist the dye

Bhairava Shiva in his monstrous aspect, the focus of a Tantric cult in 13th-century Sumatra, Bali and East Java

Bodhisattva being who has achieved enlightenment, a future Buddha who postpones his entry to nirvana to help others reach enlightenment

Bronze Age bronze working became widespread in mainland Southeast Asia during the second millennium BC – in the maritime region its introduction was accompanied by iron working towards the end of the first millennium BC

candi (Indonesian) ancient Hindu or Buddhist temple or shrine

candi bentar (Indonesian) roofless gateway, usually to an East Javanese or Balinese temple

celadon (European term) green glaze used in pottery, produced by the reaction of iron oxide in the solution to the reducing atmosphere

Chakri ruling dynasty of Thailand established in 1782 by Phra Phutta Yot Fa (Rama I), continuing to the present

Champa land of the Chams situated in what is now central Vietnam, lasting from the end of the 2nd to the start of the 19th century

chedi (Thai) originally a monument raised over relics of Buddha; later used to refer to similar monuments constructed over relics of important religious or royal figures

cili (Balinese) stylized figure representing fertility

Dai Viet polity which by the 11th century had emerged as an independent nation, in what is now north Vietnam

Devi great goddess of the Hindu religion, whose energy is known as Shakti

Dewi Sri goddess of fertility and rice in Java

Dieng plateau in Central Java, the site of a number of Hindu temples dating from the 8th to 9th centuries

dinh community house and shrine for the guardian spirit of villages in Vietnam

Dong Son site in northern Vietnam of settlement that produced bronze artefacts around 500 to 300 BC; gongs associated with the site are usually referred to as drums

Dvaravati Mon kingdom of the 6th and 7th centuries in what is now central Thailand

feng shui (lit. 'wind-water') geomancy, or the art of determining an auspicious site for a building and the arrangement within it

firasat reading of someone's character from their physical characteristics; ability to prophesy future

Funan Indian-influenced political state based in the lower reaches of the Mekong, an influential trading centre from the 1st to 5th centuries AD

Ganesha (Sanskrit) Indian god of wisdom and arts; the son of Shiva and Parvati, he has the head of an elephant

Garuda (Sanskrit) mythological winged creature with the beak and talons of a bird of prey and the upper body and arms of a man; mount of the god Vishnu; often depicted fighting with the naga, his sworn enemy

gopura rectangular tower above a gateway to a Hindu temple

Hadith body of tradition relating to the sayings and deeds of the prophet Mohammad

hajj pilgrimage to Mecca, which every Muslim should try to make

Heger typology for bronze gongs found widely in Southeast Asia, named after an Austrian scholar, Franz Heger, who classified them chronologically and on stylistic grounds

Hinduism religion including the worship of several gods and a belief in reincarnation, the law of karma, and a universal spirit

Hmong cultural and linguistic grouping of peoples living in southwest China and along the borders of Vietnam, Laos and Thailand

Hoabinhian type of hunting and gathering culture defined in terms of material culture dating from around 9000 BC and named after rock shelters in Hoa Binh, Vietnam

ider-ider (Balinese) narrative painted cloth hung around a shrine

Indravarman I (889– c. 900) founder of the first capital in the Angkor area

Iron Age iron working appeared in Southeast Asia around 600 to 400 BC; in the maritime part of the region this corresponded with the appearance of bronze technology, so there was no separate 'Iron Age'

Islam religion based on submission to a single God, Allah, whose Prophet, Mohammad, lived in the 6th and 7th centuries AD

Jambupati (Sanskrit) king humbled by the historical Buddha; also used to refer to a crowned Buddha image

Jataka (Sanskrit) collection of 547 stories about the former lives, in animal and human form, of the Buddha; each story shows a particular virtue as exemplified in the actions of the Buddha, thus serving as a model for others to follow

jian nian (Fujian) (lit. 'cut and paste') kind of mosaic using ceramic shards set in cement to form motifs

jinn genie or evil spirit

kala expression of the destructive aspect of time, personified as Mahakala, a form of Shiva, and represented in sculpture as a demonic open-mouthed face

kalan ancient Cham temple

kebe (Bima, Indonesia) supernatural power, especially to cause harm to one's enemies

kendi earthenware flask with a neck and spout, usually for drinking water

keris dagger with a double-edged blade on an asymmetrical base, found in Indonesia and the Malay world

Khmer language, dominant ethnic group and civilization of Cambodia

kiblat direction of Mecca

kitab terasul Malay guide to letter-writing

Kertanagara the last king of the 13th-century kingdom of Singasari in East Java

kraton palace, usually of Javanese ruler

Kuan Yin Chinese goddess of mercy

Kubu ethnic group, traditionally foraging forest dwellers in east central Sumatra

Kyanzittha second of the kings of Pagan (1084–1113)

Lapita ancestors of the Austronesian-speaking Melanesians; culture associated with them

linga, lingam symbolic phallus representing the life force, associated with the god Shiva (its female counterpart is the yoni)

Lopburi city in what is now central Thailand, by the 11th century a Khmer provincial capital; also Khmer art from Thailand dating from the 11th to 14th centuries

Loro Blonyo figures of a wedding couple, Dewi Sri and her consort Sadono, traditionally placed in front of the marriage bed in Java

Loro Jonggrang 9th-century Hindu temple complex at Prambanan in Central Java

Ly ruling dynasty of Vietnam (1010–1225) during whose reign independence from China was consolidated

Mahabharata Indian epic concerning the struggle for power between two related families over who should rule the kingdom of Hastina

Mahayana Buddhism major sect of Buddhism whose central tenet is that multiple bodhisattvas should encourage others to attain enlightenment

Majapahit Hindu kingdom founded in 1293 in East Java, which collapsed in the early 16th century

Mamasa Toraja ethnic group from central Sulawesi, linked to Sa'dan Toraja by ancestry

mamuli ear ornament from the island of Sumba, thought to embody the life-giving properties of female genitalia, which it resembles in shape

mandala diagrammatic representation of the cosmos showing the configuration of Buddhas and other deities, used as an aid to meditation

megamendung (Indonesian) 'great cloud', a batik motif from Cirebon derived from the canopy of one of the state coaches

Meru (or **Mahameru**) mountain at the centre of the cosmos; tower built for royal cremation ceremonies in Thailand

mihrab niche in a mosque, showing the direction of Mecca

mimbar pulpit in a mosque

Ming the first dynasty to rule over the whole of China (1368-1644)

Mon ethnic group which established many Buddhist kingdoms, in what are now Thailand and Burma, at various times from the 6th century onwards – Dvaravati, in central Thailand, is probably the best known

mudra gesture of the Buddha, in Buddhist iconography symbolic of an event in the Buddha's life

naga divine serpent living underground, symbol of the watery realm; may appear as a rainbow, linking earth and heaven

Nanyang 'Southern Ocean', mentioned in Chinese texts from the 5th century AD onwards, and referring to the Southeast Asian region

Neolithic prehistoric cultures characterized by the use of ground and polished stone implements; the period in which such cultures dominated

ngadhu shrine at the centre of villages in the Nghada region of the island of Flores honouring a male ancestor

Pali sacred language derived from Sanskrit and used in Theravada Buddhist sermons and texts

pamor (Malay/Indonesian) patterning in the blade of a keris, produced by pattern-welding

peksinagaliman composite mythical animal depicted in batik from Cirebon in Java; formed of elements from a bird, a dragon and an elephant

piso (Batak, north Sumatra) (lit. 'knife') items given by groom's family to the bride's on their wedding day

Prajnaparamita personification of wisdom in Buddhism

Prambanan village in Central Java, the site of the 9th-century Hindu temple complex of Loro Jonggrang; a number of other temples, both Hindu and Buddhist, are situated in the vicinity

prang (Thai) tall, narrow monument representing the many levels of heaven; frequently used in Khmer religious architecture and also by the Thai during the Sukhothai and Ayutthayan periods

priyayi (Javanese) belonging to upper classes

Pyu ethnic group dominant in lower Burma from the early centuries AD until around the 9th century

qilin (or **kilin**) mythical quadruped with fish scales, hooves and a horn, Chinese symbol of longevity and happiness

Qing ruling dynasty in China (1644–1911)

Quan Am in Vietnam the goddess of mercy, equivalent to the Chinese Kuan Yin

Ramayana Indian epic ('tales of Rama') known in Thailand as the Ramakien, concerning the efforts of Rama to rescue his abducted wife, with the help of Hanuman the monkey-god

rasa (Indonesian) taste, feeling

rencong Achenese dagger with curved handle

Sa'dan Toraja ethnic group from central Sulawesi

Sawankhalok city and kiln site at what is now Sisatchanalai, Thailand, which produced ceramics during the Sukhothai period

Shailendra Buddhist dynasty in Central Java, 8th to 10th centuries

Shakyamuni (lit. 'sage of the Shakyas') the historical Buddha, who was born as a member of the Shakya tribe in Nepal

Shan term applied to some Tai-speaking ethnic groups in Burma, descendants of non-Tai peoples who adopted Buddhism and other cultural elements from the Burmese

shastra Indian treatises including guidelines relating to art forms of various kinds

Shivaite pertaining to Shiva and his worship

sifat (from Arabic) characteristic, nature

Singasari kingdom in East Java (1222–1292); also a village in East Java where temples were established by Singasari rulers

Sinhalese ethnic group and language from Sri Lanka

Sri Tanjung story which appears in Old Javanese texts

Sriwijaya Buddhist trading power based in eastern Sumatra which flourished between the 7th and 12th centuries

stele upright slab, usually sculpted or inscribed

stupa bell- or dome-shaped mound covering the relics of the historical Buddha, revered monks or holy objects

subang (Malay) (lit. 'ear plugs') wing-like shapes at the upper extremities of some batu Aceh gravestones

Sudhana bodhisattva whose story is recounted in reliefs at Borobudur

Sufism mystical Islamic philosophy

Sukhothai Thai Buddhist kingdom (13th to 15th centuries), its capital and the art style associated with it; first capital of Siam

Sung ruling dynasties in China (AD 960–1279)

sura a chapter of the Qur'an

Surakarta city state founded in 1745 in what is now Solo, Central Java

Surya Hindu god, personification of the sun

Suryavarman II ruling king of Angkor (1113–1145) who was responsible for the building of Angkor Wat

Tai group of languages spoken by a number of ethnic groups in Thailand, Laos and parts of Burma; ethnic identity of such groups

taman arum (Indonesian) (lit. 'scented garden') meditation place; dwelling place of the gods

Tang Chinese dynasty which ruled from 618 to 906

Tantri tales Javanese versions of the Jataka stories

Tantrism cult of achieving cosmic union through ecstasy, often involving sexual practices and magic

Taoism Chinese religious and philosophical system based on the teachings of Lao-tze, a Chinese sage who lived around the 6th century BC

tariqat (Indonesian, from Arabic) an order of Muslim mystics; mystic guild of artisans

tau-tau (Indonesia) (lit. 'little person') life-sized mortuary effigies of the dead, placed close to burial chambers in cliffs in Toraja, Sulawesi

Tausug ethnic group, mainly Muslim, originally from the island of Jolo in the Sulu archipelago, which stretches between the major islands of the Philippines towards Borneo

Theravada Buddhism sect that focuses on the individual path to enlightenment

Tran ruling dynasty in Vietnam (1225 to 1400)

trigram a diagram made up of an arrangement of three continuous or broken lines; feng shui dials are made up of eight trigrams, representing cyclic changes in nature, arranged in a circle

Trowulan site in east Java of the capital of the Majapahit kingdom

tughra emblematic signature of Ottoman sultans

ulos (Batak, north Sumatra) cloth or gifts given by bride's side to groom's at a wedding

wali legendary apostles of Islam in Java

wat Thai Buddhist monastery, including some buildings open to lay people

wayang kulit (Indonesian) shadow theatre

Yogyakarta city state in central Java founded in 1755 following a dispute within the ruling family of the Mataram sultanate

yoni shape in the form of the female organ, in Hinduism representing female fertility

Yuan Chinese dynasty (AD 1279–1368)

Yuanshan Neolithic culture whose remains were found in Taiwany

yun Burmese term used generally for lacquer, but also specifically for the technique of making incised lacquerware

Zhou ruling Chinese dynasties (1027–221 BC)

Select Bibliography

General

Barbier, Jean-Paul (ed.), 1999. *Messages in Stone: Statues and Sculptures from Tribal Indonesia in the Collections of the Barbier-Mueller Museum.* Milan: Skira.

Bernet Kempers, A. J., 1959. *Ancient Indonesian Art.* Amsterdam: Van der Peet and Harvard University Press.

Brown, Roxanna M., 1977. *The Ceramics of South-East Asia, Their Dating and Identification.* Oxford and New York: Oxford University Press.

Coedès, George, 1968. *The Indianized States of Southeast Asia*, ed. Walter F. Vella, tr. S. B. Cowing. Honolulu: University of Hawaii Press.

Fraser-Lu, Sylvia, 1988. *Handwoven Textiles of Southeast Asia.* Singapore and Oxford: Oxford University Press.

Fraser-Lu, Sylvia, 1989. *Silverware of South-East Asia.* Singapore, Oxford and New York: Oxford University Press.

Girard-Geslan, Maud, et al, 1998. *Art of Southeast Asia.* New York: Harry N. Abrams, Inc.

Guy, John S., 1986. *Oriental Trade Ceramics in South-East Asia, Ninth to Sixteenth Centuries.* Singapore and Oxford: Oxford University Press.

Holt, Claire, 1967. *Art in Indonesia: Continuities and Change.* Ithaca, NY: Cornell University Press.

Jessup, Helen Ibbitson, 1990. *Court Arts of Indonesia.* New York: Asia Society Galleries and Harry N. Abrams, Inc.

Rodgers, Susan, and Pierre-Alain Ferrazzini, 1985. *Power and Gold: Jewelry from Indonesia, Malaysia and the Philippines.* Geneva: Musée Barbier-Müller, Prestel.

Stadtner, Donald M., 1999. *The Art of Burma: New Studies.* Mumbai: Marg Publications.

Taylor, Paul Michael (ed.), 1994. *Fragile Traditions: Indonesian Art in Jeopardy.* Honolulu: University of Hawaii Press.

Van Beek, Steve, and Luca Invernizzi Tettoni, 1991. *The Arts of Thailand.* London: Thames & Hudson.

Chapter 1

Bellwood, Peter, 1978. *Man's Conquest of the Pacific: the Prehistory of Southeast Asia and Oceania.* Auckland and London: Collins.

Bellwood, Peter, 1997. *Prehistory of the Indo-Malaysian Archipelago.* Honolulu: University of Hawaii Press.

Bernet Kempers, A. J., 1988. 'The Kettledrums of Southeast Asia: A Bronze Age World and its Aftermath.' *Modern Quaternary Research in Southeast Asia*, volume 10.

Heekeren, H. R. van, 1958. *The Bronze-Iron Age of Indonesia.* The Hague: Nijhoff.

Heine-Geldern, Robert, 1945. 'Prehistoric research in the Netherlands Indies'. In Pieter Honig and Frans Verdoorn (eds.), *Science and Scientists in the Netherlands Indies.* New York: Board for the Netherlands Indies, Surinam and Curaçao.

Higham, Charles, 1989. *The Archaeology of Mainland Southeast Asia: From 10,000 BC to the Fall of Angkor.* Cambridge: Cambridge University Press.

Higham, Charles, and Rachanie Thosarat, 1998. *Prehistoric Thailand: From Early Settlement to Sukhothai.* London: Thames & Hudson.

Lien, Chao Mei, 1991. 'The Neolithic Archaeology of Taiwan and the Peinan Excavations'. *Bulletin of the Indo-Pacific Prehistory Association*, volume 11.

Thomassen à Thuessink van der Hoop, A. N. J., 1933. *Megalithic Remains in South Sumatra*, tr. W. Shirlaw. Zutphen: W. J. Thieme.

Chapter 2

Barbier, John Paul, and Douglas Newton, 1988. *Islands and Ancestors: Indigenous Styles of Southeast Asia.* Munich: Prestel.

Chin, Lucas, and Valerie Mashman (eds.), 1991. *Sarawak Cultural Legacy: A Living Tradition.* Kuching: Society Atelier Sarawak.

De Jonge, Nico, and Toos van Dijk, 1995. *Forgotten Islands of Indonesia: The Art and Culture of the Southeast Moluccas.* Hong Kong: Periplus Editions.

Feldman, Jerome, 1985. *The Eloquent Dead: Ancestral Sculpture of Indonesia and Southeast Asia.* Los Angeles: UCLA Museum of Cultural History.

Feldman, J. A., et al, 1990. *Nias Tribal Treasures: Cosmic Reflections in Stone, Wood and Gold.* Delft: Volkenkundig Museum Nusantara.

Kartik, Kalpana, 1999. 'Images of the Dead: Megalithic Stone Tombs and Ancestor Worship in Sumba'. *Arts of Asia*, volume 29 no. 5.

Rassers, W. H., 1940. 'On the Javanese Kris'. *Bijdragen tot de Taal-, Land-, en Volkenkunde van Nederlandsche-Indie*, volume 99.

Richter, Anne, 2000. *The Jewelry of Southeast Asia*. London: Thames & Hudson.

Sellato, Bernard, 1989. *Hornbill and Dragon*. Jakarta: Elf Acquitaine Indonésie.

Taylor, Paul Michael, and Lorraine V. Aragon, 1991. *Beyond the Java Sea: Arts of Indonesia's Outer Islands*. Washington DC and New York: National Museum of Natural History, Smithsonian Institution, in association with Harry N. Abrams Inc.

Waterson, Roxana, 1990. *The Living House: An Anthropology of Architecture in South-East Asia*. Singapore, Oxford and New York: Oxford University Press.

Chapter 3

Bernet Kempers, A. J., 1991. *Monumental Bali: Introduction to Balinese Archaeology and Guide to the Monuments*. Berkeley: Periplus Editions.

Fischer, Joseph, 1994. *The Folk Art of Java*. Kuala Lumpur and Oxford: Oxford University Press.

Fischer, Joseph, and Thomas Cooper, 1998. *The Folk Art of Bali: The Narrative Tradition*. Kuala Lumpur and Oxford: Oxford University Press.

Fontein, Jan, 1990. *The Sculpture of Indonesia*. Washington DC: National Gallery of Art.

Giteau, Madeleine, 1999. *Khmer Art: The Civilisations of Angkor*. New Holland: Weatherhill.

Guillon, Emmanuel, 2001. *Cham Art: Treasures from the Da Nang Museum, Vietnam*. London: Thames & Hudson.

Lunsingh Schleurer, Pauline, and Marijke J. Klokke, 1988. *Ancient Indonesian Bronzes: A Catalogue of the Exhibition in the Rijksmuseum Amsterdam with a General Introduction*. Leiden: Brill.

Jessup, Helen Ibbitson, and Thierry Zephir, 1997. *Millennium of Glory: Sculpture of Angkor and Ancient Cambodia*. London: Thames & Hudson.

Ramseyer, Urs, 1977. *The Art and Culture of Bali*. Oxford: Oxford University Press.

Schnitger, F. M., 1937. *The Archaeology of Hindoo Sumatra*. Leiden: Brill.

Solyom, G., and B. Solyom, 1978. *The World of the Javanese Keris*. Honolulu: East-West Center.

Chapter 4

Fraser-Lu, Sylvia, 1994. *Burmese Crafts, Past and Present*. Kuala Lumpur: Oxford University Press.

Frédéric, Louis, and Jean-Louis Nou, 1996. *Borobudur*. New York: Abbeville Press.

Ginsburg, Henry, 2000. *Thai Art and Culture: Historic Manuscripts from Western Collections*. London: British Museum Press.

Gosling, Betty, 1991. *Sukhothai: Its History, Culture and Art*. Oxford and Singapore: Oxford University Press.

Green, Alexandra, and T. Richard Blurton (eds.), 2003. *Burma: Art and Archaeology*. London: British Museum Press.

Nguyen-Long, Kerry, 1999. 'Vietnamese Blue and White Ceramics, Fourteenth to Seventeenth Centuries.' *Arts of Asia*, volume 29 no. 5.

Ringis, Rita, 1990. *Thai Temples and Temple Murals*. Singapore, Oxford and New York: Oxford University Press.

Stargardt, Janice, 1991. *The Ancient Pyu of Burma*. Cambridge: Cambridge University Press.

Strachan, Paul, 1989. *Pagan: Art and Architecture of Old Burma*. Whiting Bay: Kiscadale.

Stratton, Carol, and Miriam McNair Scott, 1981. *The Art of Sukhothai: Thailand's Golden Age from the Mid-Thirteenth to the Mid-Fifteenth Centuries*. Kuala Lumpur and Oxford: Oxford University Press.

Chapter 5

Gallop, Annabel Teh, 1991. *Golden Letters: Writing Traditions of Indonesia*. London and Jakarta: British Library and the Lontar Foundation.

Gallop, Annabel Teh, and E. U. Kratz, 1994. *The Legacy of the Malay Letter*. London: British Library.

Harsrinuksmo, Bambang, and S. Lumintu (eds.), 1988. *Keris dan Senjata Tradisional Indonesia Lainnya*. Jakarta: Cipta Adi Pustaka.

Kerlogue, F. G., 2001. 'Islamic Talismans: The Calligraphy Batiks' in Itie van Hout (ed.), *Batik Drawn in Wax*. Amsterdam: Royal Tropical Institute.

Lambourn, E., 2004. 'Rethinking Batu Aceh'. *Indonesia and the Malay World*, volume 32 (June).

Noor, Farish A., and Khoo, E., 2003. *Spirit of Wood: The Art of Malay Woodcarving*. Hong Kong: Periplus Editions.

O'Neill, Hugh, 1994. 'South-East Asia' in M. Frishman & H. Khan (eds.), The Mosque: History, Architectural Development and Regional Diversity. London: Thames & Hudson.

Othman Mohd Yatim, 1988. Batu Aceh: Early Islamic Gravestones in Peninsular Malaysia. Kuala Lumpur: Persatuan Muzium Malaysia.

Othman Mohd Yatim, 1989.Warisan Kesenian Dalam Tamadun Islam. Kuala Lumpur: Dewan Bahasa dan Pustaka Kementerian Pendidikan Malaysia.

Shariffuddin, P. M., 1969. 'Brunei Cannon'. Brunei Museum Journal, volume 1 no. 1.

Sheppard, Mubin, 1972. Taman Indera: A Royal Pleasure Ground. Kuala Lumpur: Oxford University Press.

Sulaiman Othman, Dato' Haji, et al, 1994. The Crafts of Malaysia. Singapore: Editions Didier Millet.

Chapter 6

Duggan, G., 2001. 'The Chinese Batiks of Java'. In Itie van Hout (ed.), Batik: Drawn in Wax. Amsterdam: Royal Tropical Institute.

Fraser-Lu, Sylvia, 2000. Burmese Lacquerware. Bangkok: White Orchid Books.

Ho Wing Meng, 1983. Straits Chinese Porcelain: A Collector's Guide. Singapore: Times Books International.

Ho Wing Meng, 1984. Straits Chinese Silver: A Collector's Guide. Singapore: Times Books International.

Ho Wing Meng, 1987. Straits Chinese Beadwork and Embroidery. Singapore: Times Books International.

Isaacs, Ralph, and T. Richard Blurton. 2000. Visions from the Golden Land: Burma and the Art of Lacquer. London: British Museum Press.

Khoo Joo Ee, 1996. The Straits Chinese: A Cultural History. Amsterdam: Pepin Press.

Kohl, David G., 1984. Chinese Architecture in the Straits Settlements and Western Malaya: Temples, Kongsis, and Houses. Kuala Lumpur. Heinemann.

Stevenson, John, and John Guy, 1997. Vietnamese Ceramics: A Separate Tradition. Chicago: Art Media Resources.

Chapter 7

De Hartingh, Bertrand, et al, 1998. Vietnam: Plastic and Visual Arts from 1925 to Our Time. Brussels: La Lettre Volée.

Djelantik, A. A. M., 1986. Balinese Paintings. Singapore and Oxford: Oxford University Press.

Fenema, Joyce van, et al, 1996. Southeast Asian Art Today. Singapore: Roeder Publications.

Fischer, Joseph (ed.), 1990. Modern Indonesian Art: Three Generations of Tradition and Change 1945–1990. Jakarta and New York: Panitia Pameran KIAS and Festival of Indonesia.

Gatbauton, Juan T., Jeannie E. Javelosa and Lourdes Ruth R. Roa (eds.), 1992. Art Philippines. Manila: Crucible Workshop.

Phillips, Herbert P., 1992. The Integrative Art of Modern Thailand. Berkeley: Lowie Museum of Anthropology, University of California.

Piyadasa, Redza, 1998. Rupa Malaysia: A Decade of Art 1987–1997. Kuala Lumpur: National Art Gallery of Malaysia.

Poshyananda, Apinan, 1992. Modern Art in Thailand: Nineteenth and Twentieth Centuries. Singapore and New York: Oxford University Press.

Sabapathy, T. K. (ed.), 1994. Vision and Idea; Re-looking Modern Malaysian Art. Kuala Lumpur: National Art Gallery of Malaysia.

Santa Maris, Felice Prudente (ed.), 1998. Discovering Philippine Art in Spain. Manila: Department of Foreign Affairs/National Centennial Commission-Committee on International Relations.

Thai Contemporary Art 2000. Bangkok: Art Centre, Silpakorn University.

Ushiroshoji, Masahiro, and Toshiko Rawanchaikul (eds), 1997. The Birth of Modern Art in Southeast Asia: Artists and Movements. Fukuoka City: Fukuoka Art Museum.

Wright, Astri, 1994. Soul, Spirit and Mountain: Preoccupations of Contemporary Indonesian Painters. Kuala Lumpur, New York and Oxford: Oxford University Press.

Illustration List

170 Fua Haribhitak, *Composition*, 1955, oil on canvas, 88 × 65 cm. Silpa Bhirasri Memorial Museum, Bangkok

171 Prasong Padamanya, *Wat Pho*, 1958, tempura, 87 × 107 cm. National Gallery of Art, Bangkok

172 Montien Boonma, *Water*, 1991, soil pigment on *saa* paper, terracotta jars with smoke and soil pigment, 380 × 450 × 40 cm. Collection of the artist, Bangkok

173 Sutee Kunavichyanant, *White Elephant*, 1999, latex rubber, air balloon, hose, 120 × 257 × 380 cm. Silpakorn University Art Centre, Bangkok. Courtesy of the artist.

174 Nguyen Gia Tri, *Women*, 1951–56, Laquer, 51 × 72 cm. Collection Duc Minh, Ho Chi Minh City

175 Tran Van Can, *Militia Women in the Coastal Zone*, 1960, oil on canvas, 60 × 82 cm. Fine Arts National Museum, Hanoi

176 Bui Xuan Phai, *Cheo*, 1987, poster colours, 21 × 16 cm. Collection Pham van Bong, Hanoi

177 Syed Ahmad Jamal, *The Bait*, 1959, oil on board, 122 × 154 cm. The Collection of The National Art Gallery Malaysia

178 Yeoh Jin Leng, *Padi Field, Orchard, Hill, Sky*, 1963, oil on canvas, 102 × 83 cm. The Collection of The National Art Gallery Malaysia

179 Kelvin Chap Kok Leong, *Belawing, Keramen, Mamat*, 1995, mixed media, 141 × 57 × 51 cm. The Collection of The National Art Gallery Malaysia

180 Mastura Abdul Rahman, *Interior no. 29*, 1987, mixed oil paint, collage on plywood construction and plant twigs, 112 × 115.5 cm. The Collection of The National Art Gallery Malaysia

181 Victorio Edades, *The Builders*, 1928, oil on board. Cultural Center of the Philippines Collection

182 Fernando Amorsolo, *Rice Field*, 1952, oil on canvas laid down on board. Photo Christies Images

183 Manuel Rodrigues Jnr., *Tinggians*, 1978, painted and dyed cloth, 153.1 × 127 cm. Cultural Center of the Philippines Collection

Acknowledgments
I am very grateful to all the friends and colleagues in Europe and in Southeast Asia who have helped with comments, advice and the generous offer of photographs for this book. I would also like to thank the Southeast Asia committee of the British Academy for providing funding to support some of the research.

Index

PENGUIN PLAYS

"MASTER HAROLD" . . . AND THE BOYS

Athol Fugard was born in 1932 in Cape Province, South
Africa. An actor and a director as well as a writer, he is the
author of *A Lesson from Aloes* (winner of the New York
Drama Critics' Circle Award for Best Play of 1980),
*Boesman & Lena, Sizwe Bansi Is Dead, The Island, The
Bloodknot,* and other plays. He has also written a novel,
Tsotsi, and the film scripts *The Guest* and *Marigolds in Au-
gust.*

"MASTER HAROLD"
...and the boys

Athol Fugard

PENGUIN BOOKS

for Sam and H.D.F.

PENGUIN BOOKS
Published by the Penguin Group
Penguin Books USA Inc.,
375 Hudson Street, New York, New York 10014, U.S.A.
Penguin Books Ltd, 27 Wrights Lane, London W8 5TZ, England
Penguin Books Australia Ltd, Ringwood, Victoria, Australia
Penguin Books Canada Ltd, 10 Alcorn Avenue,
Toronto, Ontario, Canada M4V 3B2
Penguin Books (N.Z.) Ltd, 182–190 Wairau Road, Auckland 10, New Zealand

Penguin Books Ltd, Registered Offices:
Harmondsworth, Middlesex, England

First published in the United States of America by
Alfred A. Knopf, Inc., 1982
Published by Viking Penguin Inc. 1984

25 27 29 30 28 26

LIBRARY OF CONGRESS CATALOGING IN PUBLICATION DATA
Fugard, Athol.
"Master Harold"—and the boys.
I. Title.
PR9360.3.F8M3 1984   822   84-1008
ISBN 0 14 048.187 7

CAUTION: Professionals and amateurs are hereby notified that this play, being fully protected under the copyright laws of the United States of America, the British Commonwealth, including the Dominion of Canada and all other countries which are members of the Berne and Universal Copyright Conventions, is subject to royalty. All rights, including but not limited to professional, amateur publication, motion picture, recitation, public readings, radio and television broadcasting, and the right of translation into foreign languages, are expressly reserved to the Author. All inquiries concerning rights should be addressed to the William Morris Agency, 1350 Avenue of the Americas, New York, New York 10019.

Originally produced in 1982 by The Yale Repertory Theatre,
New Haven, Connecticut.
Originally produced on Broadway by The Shubert Organization,
Freydberg/Bloch Productions, Dasha Epstein,
Emanuel Azenberg, and David Geffen.

Printed in the United States of America
Set in Scotch

"MASTER
HAROLD"
...and the boys

The first performance of

"MASTER HAROLD"
. . . and the boys

was given at the Yale Repertory
Theatre on March 12, 1982,
with the following cast:

HALLY	Željko Ivanek
SAM	Zakes Mokae
WILLIE	Danny Glover

The production was directed by the author.
Sets were designed by Jane Clark.
Costumes were designed by Sheila McLamb.
Lights were designed by David Noling.

In New York, the role of Hally was played
by Lonny Price.

The St. George's Park Tea Room on a wet and windy Port Elizabeth afternoon.

Tables and chairs have been cleared and are stacked on one side except for one which stands apart with a single chair. On this table a knife, fork, spoon and side plate in anticipation of a simple meal, together with a pile of comic books.

Other elements: a serving counter with a few stale cakes under glass and a not very impressive display of sweets, cigarettes and cool drinks, etc.; a few cardboard advertising handouts—Cadbury's Chocolate, Coca-Cola—and a blackboard on which an untrained hand has chalked up the prices of Tea, Coffee, Scones, Milkshakes—all flavors—and Cool Drinks; a few sad ferns in pots; a telephone; an old-style jukebox.

There is an entrance on one side and an exit into a kitchen on the other.

Leaning on the solitary table, his head cupped in one hand as he pages through one of the comic books, is SAM. A black man in his mid-forties. He wears the white coat of a waiter. Behind him on his knees, mopping down the

floor with a bucket of water and a rag, is WILLIE. Also black and about the same age as Sam. He has his sleeves and trousers rolled up.

The year: 1950

WILLIE   (*Singing as he works*)
"She was scandalizin' my name,
She took my money
She called me honey
But she was scandalizin' my name.
Called it love but was playin' a game . . ."
   (*He gets up and moves the bucket. Stands thinking for a moment, then, raising his arms to hold an imaginary partner, he launches into an intricate ballroom dance step. Although a mildly comic figure, he reveals a reasonable degree of accomplishment*)
Hey, Sam.
   (SAM, *absorbed in the comic book, does not respond*)
Hey, Boet Sam!
   (SAM *looks up*)
I'm getting it. The quickstep. Look now and tell me. (*He repeats the step*)   Well?

SAM   (*Encouragingly*)   Show me again.

WILLIE   Okay, count for me.

SAM   Ready?

WILLIE   Ready.

SAM   Five, six, seven, eight . . . (WILLIE *starts to dance*)   A-n-d one two three four . . . and one two three four. . . .   (*Ad libbing as* WILLIE *dances*) Your shoulders, Willie . . . your shoulders! Don't look down! Look happy, Willie! Relax, Willie!

WILLIE   (*Desperate but still dancing*)   I am relax.

SAM   No, you're not.

WILLIE   (*He falters*)   Ag no man, Sam! Mustn't talk. You make me make mistakes.

SAM   But you're too stiff.

WILLIE   Yesterday I'm not straight . . . today I'm too stiff!

SAM   Well, you are. You asked me and I'm telling you.

WILLIE   Where?

SAM   Everywhere. Try to glide through it.

WILLIE   Glide?

SAM   Ja, make it smooth. And give it more style. It must look like you're enjoying yourself.

WILLIE   (*Emphatically*)   I wasn't.

SAM   Exactly.

WILLIE   How can I enjoy myself? Not straight, too stiff and now it's also glide, give it more style, make it smooth. . . . Haai! Is hard to remember all those things, Boet Sam.

SAM   That's your trouble. You're trying too hard.

WILLIE   I try hard because it *is* hard.

SAM   But don't let me see it. The secret is to make it look easy. Ballroom must look happy, Willie, not like hard work. It must . . . Ja! . . . it must look like romance.

WILLIE   Now another one! What's romance?

SAM   Love story with happy ending. A handsome man in tails, and in his arms, smiling at him, a beautiful lady in evening dress!

WILLIE   Fred Astaire, Ginger Rogers.

SAM   You got it. Tapdance or ballroom, it's the same. Romance. In two weeks' time when the judges look at you and Hilda, they must see a man and a woman who

are dancing their way to a happy ending. What I saw was you holding her like you were frightened she was going to run away.

WILLIE   Ja! Because that is what she wants to do! I got no romance left for Hilda anymore, Boet Sam.

SAM   Then pretend. When you put your arms around Hilda, imagine she is Ginger Rogers.

WILLIE   With no teeth? You try.

SAM   Well, just remember, there's only two weeks left.

WILLIE   I know, I know! (*To the jukebox*) I do it better with music. You got sixpence for Sarah Vaughan?

SAM   That's a slow foxtrot. You're practicing the quick-step.

WILLIE   I'll practice slow foxtrot.

SAM   (*Shaking his head*) It's your turn to put money in the jukebox.

WILLIE   I only got bus fare to go home. (*He returns disconsolately to his work*) Love story and happy ending! She's doing it all right, Boet Sam, but is not me she's giving happy endings. Fuckin' whore! Three nights now she doesn't come practice. I wind up gramophone, I get record ready and I sit and wait. What happens? Nothing. Ten o'clock I start dancing with my pillow. You try and practice romance by yourself, Boet Sam. Struesgod, she doesn't come tonight I take back my dress and ballroom shoes and I find me new partner. Size twenty-six. Shoes size seven. And now she's also making trouble for me with the baby again. Reports me to Child Wellfed, that I'm not giving her money. She lies! Every week I am giving her money for milk. And how do I know is my baby? Only his hair looks like me. She's fucking around all the time I turn my back. Hilda Samuels is a bitch! (*Pause*) Hey, Sam!

SAM   Ja.

WILLIE   You listening?

SAM   Ja.

WILLIE   So what you say?

SAM   About Hilda?

WILLIE   Ja.

SAM   When did you last give her a hiding?

WILLIE   (*Reluctantly*)   Sunday night.

SAM   And today is Thursday.

WILLIE   (*He knows what's coming*)   Okay.

SAM   Hiding on Sunday night, then Monday, Tuesday and Wednesday she doesn't come to practice . . . and you are asking me why?

WILLIE   I said okay, Boet Sam!

SAM   You hit her too much. One day she's going to leave you for good.

WILLIE   So? She makes me the hell-in too much.

SAM   (*Emphasizing his point*)   *Too* much and *too* hard. You had the same trouble with Eunice.

WILLIE   Because she also make the hell-in, Boet Sam. She never got the steps right. Even the waltz.

SAM   Beating her up every time she makes a mistake in the waltz?   (*Shaking his head*)   No, Willie! That takes the pleasure out of ballroom dancing.

WILLIE   Hilda is not too bad with the waltz, Boet Sam. Is the quickstep where the trouble starts.

SAM   (*Teasing him gently*)   How's your pillow with the quickstep?

WILLIE   (*Ignoring the tease*)   Good! And why? Be-

cause it got no legs. That's her trouble. She can't move them quick enough, Boet Sam. I start the record and before halfway Count Basie is already winning. Only time we catch up with him is when gramophone runs down.

(SAM *laughs*)

Haaikona, Boet Sam, is not funny.

SAM   (*Snapping his fingers*)   I got it! Give her a handicap.

WILLIE   What's that?

SAM   Give her a ten-second start and then let Count Basie go. Then I put my money on her. Hot favorite in the Ballroom Stakes: Hilda Samuels ridden by Willie Malopo.

WILLIE   (*Turning away*)   I'm not talking to you no more.

SAM   (*Relenting*)   Sorry, Willie . . .

WILLIE   It's finish between us.

SAM   Okay, okay . . . I'll stop.

WILLIE   You can also fuck off.

SAM   Willie, listen! I want to help you!

WILLIE   No more jokes?

SAM   I promise.

WILLIE   Okay. Help me.

SAM   (*His turn to hold an imaginary partner*)   Look and learn. Feet together. Back straight. Body relaxed. Right hand placed gently in the small of her back and wait for the music. Don't start worrying about making mistakes or the judges or the other competitors. It's just you, Hilda and the music, and you're going to have a good time. What Count Basie do you play?

WILLIE "You the cream in my coffee, you the salt in my stew."

SAM Right. Give it to me in strict tempo.

WILLIE Ready?

SAM Ready.

WILLIE A-n-d . . . (*Singing*)
"You the cream in my coffee.
You the salt in my stew.
You will always be my
    necessity.
I'd be lost without
    you. . . ." (*etc.*)
(SAM *launches into the quickstep. He is obviously a much more accomplished dancer than* WILLIE. HALLY *enters. A seventeen-year-old white boy. Wet raincoat and school case. He stops and watches* SAM. *The demonstration comes to an end with a flourish. Applause from* HALLY *and* WILLIE)

HALLY Bravo! No question about it. First place goes to Mr. Sam Semela.

WILLIE (*In total agreement*) You was gliding with style, Boet Sam.

HALLY (*Cheerfully*) How's it, chaps?

SAM Okay, Hally.

WILLIE (*Springing to attention like a soldier and saluting*) At your service, Master Harold!

HALLY Not long to the big event, hey!

SAM Two weeks.

HALLY You nervous?

SAM No.

HALLY Think you stand a chance?

SAM   Let's just say I'm ready to go out there and dance.

HALLY   It looked like it. What about you, Willie?
    (WILLIE *groans*)
    What's the matter?

SAM   He's got leg trouble.   •

HALLY   (*Innocently*)   Oh, sorry to hear that, Willie.

WILLIE   Boet Sam! You promised.   (WILLIE *returns to his work*)
    (HALLY *deposits his school case and takes off his raincoat. His clothes are a little neglected and untidy: black blazer with school badge, gray flannel trousers in need of an ironing, khaki shirt and tie, black shoes.* SAM *has fetched a towel for* HALLY *to dry his hair*)

HALLY   God, what a lousy bloody day. It's coming down cats and dogs out there. Bad for business, chaps . . . (*Conspiratorial whisper*)   . . . but it also means we're in for a nice quiet afternoon.

SAM   You can speak loud. Your Mom's not here.

HALLY   Out shopping?

SAM   No. The hospital.

HALLY   But it's Thursday. There's no visiting on Thursday afternoons. Is my Dad okay?

SAM   Sounds like it. In fact, I think he's going home.

HALLY   (*Stopped short by* SAM'S *remark*)   What do you mean?

SAM   The hospital phoned.

HALLY   To say what?

SAM   I don't know. I just heard your Mom talking.

HALLY   So what makes you say he's going home?

SAM   It sounded as if they were telling her to come and fetch him.

(HALLY *thinks about what* SAM *has said for a few seconds*)

HALLY   When did she leave?

SAM   About an hour ago. She said she would phone you. Want to eat?
 (HALLY *doesn't respond*)
Hally, want your lunch?

HALLY   I suppose so. (*His mood has changed*) What's on the menu? . . . as if I don't know.

SAM   Soup, followed by meat pie and gravy.

HALLY   Today's?

SAM   No.

HALLY   And the soup?

SAM   Nourishing pea soup.

HALLY   Just the soup. (*The pile of comic books on the table*) And these?

SAM   For your Dad. Mr. Kempston brought them.

HALLY   You haven't been reading them, have you?

SAM   Just looking.

HALLY   (*Examining the comics*) *Jungle Jim . . . Batman and Robin . . . Tarzan* . . . God, what rubbish! Mental pollution. Take them away.
 (SAM *exits waltzing into the kitchen.* HALLY *turns to* WILLIE)

HALLY   Did you hear my Mom talking on the telephone, Willie?

WILLIE   No, Master Hally. I was at the back.

HALLY   And she didn't say anything to you before she left?

WILLIE   She said I must clean the floors.

HALLY   I mean about my Dad.

WILLIE   She didn't say nothing to me about him, Master Hally.

HALLY   (*With conviction*)   No! It can't be. They said he needed at least another three weeks of treatment. Sam's definitely made a mistake.   (*Rummages through his school case, finds a book and settles down at the table to read*)   So, Willie!

WILLIE   Yes, Master Hally! Schooling okay today?

HALLY   Yes, okay. . . .   (*He thinks about it*)   . . . No, not really. Ag, what's the difference? I don't care. And Sam says you've got problems.

WILLIE   Big problems.

HALLY   Which leg is sore?
  (WILLIE *groans*)
Both legs.

WILLIE   There is nothing wrong with my legs. Sam is just making jokes.

HALLY   So then you *will* be in the competition.

WILLIE   Only if I can find me a partner.

HALLY   But what about Hilda?

SAM   (*Returning with a bowl of soup*)   She's the one who's got trouble with her legs.

HALLY   What sort of trouble, Willie?

SAM   From the way he describes it, I think the lady has gone a bit lame.

HALLY   Good God! Have you taken her to see a doctor?

SAM   I think a vet would be better.

HALLY   What do you mean?

SAM   What do you call it again when a racehorse goes very fast?

HALLY   Gallop?

SAM   That's it!

WILLIE   Boet Sam!

HALLY   "A gallop down the homestretch to the winning post." But what's that got to do with Hilda?

SAM   Count Basie always gets there first.
    (WILLIE *lets fly with his slop rag. It misses* SAM *and hits* HALLY)

HALLY   (*Furious*)   For Christ's sake, Willie! What the hell do you think you're doing!

WILLIE   Sorry, Master Hally, but it's him. . . .

HALLY   Act your bloody age!   (*Hurls the rag back at* WILLIE)   Cut out the nonsense now and get on with your work. And you too, Sam. Stop fooling around.
    (SAM *moves away*)
No. Hang on. I haven't finished! Tell me exactly what my Mom said.

SAM   I have. "When Hally comes, tell him I've gone to the hospital and I'll phone him."

HALLY   She didn't say anything about taking my Dad home?

SAM   No. It's just that when she was talking on the phone . . .

HALLY   (*Interrupting him*)   No, Sam. They can't be discharging him. She would have said so if they were. In any case, we saw him last night and he wasn't in good shape at all. Staff nurse even said there was talk about taking more X-rays. And now suddenly today he's better? If anything, it sounds more like a bad turn to me . . . which I sincerely hope it isn't. Hang on . . . how long ago did you say she left?

SAM   Just before two . . . (*His wrist watch*) . . . hour and a half.

HALLY   I know how to settle it.   (*Behind the counter to the telephone. Talking as he dials*)   Let's give her ten minutes to get to the hospital, ten minutes to load him up, another ten, at the most, to get home and another ten to get him inside. Forty minutes. They should have been home for at least half an hour already.   (*Pause— he waits with the receiver to his ear*)   No reply, chaps. And you know why? Because she's at his bedside in hospital helping him pull through a bad turn. You definitely heard wrong.

SAM   Okay.
    (*As far as* HALLY *is concerned, the matter is settled. He returns to his table, sits down and divides his attention between the book and his soup.* SAM *is at his school case and picks up a textbook*)
    Modern Graded Mathematics for Standards Nine and Ten.   (*Opens it at random and laughs at something he sees*)   Who is this supposed to be?

HALLY   Old fart-face Prentice.

SAM   Teacher?

HALLY   Thinks he is. And believe me, that is not a bad likeness.

SAM   Has he seen it?

HALLY   Yes.

SAM   What did he say?

HALLY   Tried to be clever, as usual. Said I was no Leonardo da Vinci and that bad art had to be punished. So, six of the best, and his are bloody good.

SAM   On your bum?

HALLY   Where else? The days when I got them on my hands are gone forever, Sam.

SAM   With your trousers down!

HALLY   No. He's not quite that barbaric.

SAM   That's the way they do it in jail.

HALLY   (*Flicker of morbid interest*)   Really?

SAM   Ja. When the magistrate sentences you to "strokes with a light cane."

HALLY   Go on.

SAM   They make you lie down on a bench. One policeman pulls down your trousers and holds your ankles, another one pulls your shirt over your head and holds your arms . . .

HALLY   Thank you! That's enough.

SAM   . . . and the one that gives you the strokes talks to you gently and for a long time between each one. (*He laughs*)

HALLY   I've heard enough, Sam! Jesus! It's a bloody awful world when you come to think of it. People can be real bastards.

SAM   That's the way it is, Hally.

HALLY   It doesn't *have* to be that way. There is something called progress, you know. We don't exactly burn people at the stake anymore.

SAM   Like Joan of Arc.

HALLY   Correct. If she was captured today, she'd be given a fair trial.

SAM   And then the death sentence.

HALLY   (*A world-weary sigh*)   I know, I know! I oscillate between hope and despair for this world as well, Sam. But things will change, you wait and see. One day somebody is going to get up and give history a kick up the backside and get it going again.

SAM   Like who?

HALLY   (*After thought*)   They're called social re-

formers. Every age, Sam, has got its social reformer. My history book is full of them.

SAM   So where's ours?

HALLY   Good question. And I hate to say it, but the answer is: I don't know. Maybe he hasn't even been born yet. Or is still only a babe in arms at his mother's breast. God, what a thought.

SAM   So we just go on waiting.

HALLY   Ja, looks like it.   (*Back to his soup and the book*)

SAM   (*Reading from the textbook*)   "Introduction: In some mathematical problems only the magnitude . . ." (*He mispronounces the word "magnitude"*)

HALLY   (*Correcting him without looking up*)   Magnitude.

SAM   What's it mean?

HALLY   How big it is. The size of the thing.

SAM   (*Reading*)   ". . . magnitude of the quantities is of importance. In other problems we need to know whether these quantities are negative or positive. For example, whether there is a debit or credit bank balance . . ."

HALLY   Whether you're broke or not.

SAM   ". . . whether the temperature is above or below Zero . . ."

HALLY   Naught degrees. Cheerful state of affairs! No cash and you're freezing to death. Mathematics won't get you out of that one.

SAM   "All these quantities are called . . ."   (*Spelling the word*)   . . . s-c-a-l . . .

HALLY   Scalars.

SAM Scalars! (*Shaking his head with a laugh*) You understand all that?

HALLY (*Turning a page*) No. And I don't intend to try.

SAM So what happens when the exams come?

HALLY Failing a maths exam isn't the end of the world, Sam. How many times have I told you that examination results don't measure intelligence?

SAM I would say about as many times as you've failed one of them.

HALLY (*Mirthlessly*) Ha, ha, ha.

SAM (*Simultaneously*) Ha, ha, ha.

HALLY Just remember Winston Churchill didn't do particularly well at school.

SAM You've also told me that one many times.

HALLY Well, it just so happens to be the truth.

SAM (*Enjoying the word*) Magnitude! Magnitude! Show me how to use it.

HALLY (*After thought*) An intrepid social reformer will not be daunted by the magnitude of the task he has undertaken.

SAM (*Impressed*) Couple of jaw-breakers in there!

HALLY I gave you three for the price of one. Intrepid, daunted and magnitude. I did that once in an exam. Put five of the words I had to explain in one sentence. It was half a page long.

SAM Well, I'll put my money on you in the English exam.

HALLY Piece of cake. Eighty percent without even trying.

SAM   (*Another textbook from* HALLY's *case*)   And history?

HALLY   So-so. I'll scrape through. In the fifties if I'm lucky.

SAM   You didn't do too badly last year.

HALLY   Because we had World War One. That at least had some action. You try to find that in the South African Parliamentary system.

SAM   (*Reading from the history textbook*) "Napoleon and the principle of equality." Hey! This sounds interesting. "After concluding peace with Britain in 1802, Napoleon used a brief period of calm to in-sti-tute . . ."

HALLY   Introduce.

SAM   ". . . many reforms. Napoleon regarded all people as equal before the law and wanted them to have equal opportunities for advancement. All ves-ti-ges of the feu-dal system with its oppression of the poor were abolished." Vestiges, feudal system and abolished. I'm all right on oppression.

HALLY   I'm thinking. He swept away . . . abolished . . . the last remains . . . vestiges . . . of the bad old days . . . feudal system.

SAM   Ha! There's the social reformer we're waiting for. He sounds like a man of some magnitude.

HALLY   I'm not so sure about that. It's a damn good title for a book, though. A man of magnitude!

SAM   He sounds pretty big to me, Hally.

HALLY   Don't confuse historical significance with greatness. But maybe I'm being a bit prejudiced. Have a look in there and you'll see he's two chapters long. And hell! . . . has he only got dates, Sam, all of which you've got to remember! This campaign and that cam-

paign, and then, because of all the fighting, the next thing is we get Peace Treaties all over the place. And what's the end of the story? Battle of Waterloo, which he loses. Wasn't worth it. No, I don't know about him as a man of magnitude.

SAM   Then who would you say was?

HALLY   To answer that, we need a definition of greatness, and I suppose that would be somebody who . . . somebody who benefited all mankind.

SAM   Right. But like who?

HALLY   (*He speaks with total conviction*) Charles Darwin. Remember him? That big book from the library. *The Origin of the Species.*

SAM   Him?

HALLY   Yes. For his Theory of Evolution.

SAM   You didn't finish it.

HALLY   I ran out of time. I didn't finish it because my two weeks was up. But I'm going to take it out again after I've digested what I read. It's safe. I've hidden it away in the Theology section. Nobody ever goes in there. And anyway who are you to talk? You hardly even looked at it.

SAM   I tried. I looked at the chapters in the beginning and I saw one called "The Struggle for an Existence." Ah ha, I thought. At last! But what did I get? Something called the mistiltoe which needs the apple tree and there's too many seeds and all are going to die except one . . . ! No, Hally.

HALLY   (*Intellectually outraged*) What do you mean, No! The poor man had to start somewhere. For God's sake, Sam, he revolutionized science. Now we know.

SAM   What?

HALLY   Where we come from and what it all means.

SAM   And that's a benefit to mankind? Anyway, I still don't believe it.

HALLY   God, you're impossible. I showed it to you in black and white.

SAM   Doesn't mean I got to believe it.

HALLY   It's the likes of you that kept the Inquisition in business. It's called bigotry. Anyway, that's my man of magnitude. Charles Darwin! Who's yours?

SAM   (*Without hesitation*)   Abraham Lincoln.

HALLY   I might have guessed as much. Don't get sentimental, Sam. You've never been a slave, you know. And anyway we freed your ancestors here in South Africa long before the Americans. But if you want to thank somebody on their behalf, do it to Mr. William Wilberforce. Come on. Try again. I want a real genius. (*Now enjoying himself, and so is* SAM. HALLY *goes behind the counter and helps himself to a chocolate*)

SAM   William Shakespeare.

HALLY   (*No enthusiasm*)   Oh. So you're also one of them, are you? You're basing that opinion on only one play, you know. You've only read my *Julius Caesar* and even I don't understand half of what they're talking about. They should do what they did with the old Bible: bring the language up to date.

SAM   That's all you've got. It's also the only one *you've* read.

HALLY   I know. I admit it. That's why I suggest we reserve our judgment until we've checked up on a few others. I've got a feeling, though, that by the end of this year one is going to be enough for me, and I can give you the names of twenty-nine other chaps in the Standard Nine class of the Port Elizabeth Technical College who feel the same. But if you want him, you can have him. My turn now. (*Pacing*)   This is a

damned good exercise, you know! It started off looking like a simple question and here it's got us really probing into the intellectual heritage of our civilization.

SAM So who is it going to be?

HALLY My next man . . . and he gets the title on two scores: social reform and literary genius . . . is Leo Nikolaevich Tolstoy.

SAM That Russian.

HALLY Correct. Remember the picture of him I showed you?

SAM With the long beard.

HALLY (*Trying to look like Tolstoy*) And those burning, visionary eyes. My God, the face of a social prophet if ever I saw one! And remember my words when I showed it to you? Here's a *man*, Sam!

SAM Those were words, Hally.

HALLY Not many intellectuals are prepared to shovel manure with the peasants and then go home and write a "little book" called *War and Peace*. Incidentally, Sam, he was somebody else who, to quote, ". . . did not distinguish himself scholastically."

SAM Meaning?

HALLY He was also no good at school.

SAM Like you and Winston Churchill.

HALLY (*Mirthlessly*) Ha, ha, ha.

SAM (*Simultaneously*) Ha, ha, ha.

HALLY Don't get clever, Sam. That man freed his serfs of his own free will.

SAM No argument. He was a somebody, all right. I accept him.

HALLY I'm sure Count Tolstoy will be very pleased to

hear that. Your turn. Shoot. (*Another chocolate from behind the counter*)   I'm waiting, Sam.

SAM   I've got him.

HALLY   Good. Submit your candidate for examination.

SAM   Jesus.

HALLY   (*Stopped dead in his tracks*)   Who?

SAM   Jesus Christ.

HALLY   Oh, come on, Sam!

SAM   The Messiah.

HALLY   Ja, but still . . . No, Sam. Don't let's get started on religion. We'll just spend the whole afternoon arguing again. Suppose I turn around and say Mohammed?

SAM   All right.

HALLY   You can't have them both on the same list!

SAM   Why not? You like Mohammed, I like Jesus.

HALLY   I *don't* like Mohammed. I never have. I was merely being hypothetical. As far as I'm concerned, the Koran is as bad as the Bible. No. Religion is out! I'm not going to waste my time again arguing with you about the existence of God. You know perfectly well I'm an atheist . . . and I've got homework to do.

SAM   Okay, I take him back.

HALLY   You've got time for one more name.

SAM   (*After thought*)   I've got one I know we'll agree on. A simple straightforward great Man of Magnitude . . . and no arguments. And *he* really *did* benefit all mankind.

HALLY   I wonder. After your last contribution I'm beginning to doubt whether anything in the way of an intellectual agreement is possible between the two of us. Who is he?

SAM   Guess.

HALLY   Socrates? Alexandre Dumas? Karl Marx? Dostoevsky? Nietzsche?
(SAM *shakes his head after each name*)
Give me a clue.

SAM   The letter P is important . . .

HALLY   Plato!

SAM   . . . and his name begins with an F.

HALLY   I've got it. Freud and Psychology.

SAM   No. I didn't understand him.

HALLY   That makes two of us.

SAM   Think of mouldy apricot jam.

HALLY   (*After a delighted laugh*)   Penicillin and Sir Alexander Fleming! And the title of the book: *The Microbe Hunters*. (*Delighted*)   Splendid, Sam! Splendid. For once we are in total agreement. The major breakthrough in medical science in the Twentieth Century. If it wasn't for him, we might have lost the Second World War. It's deeply gratifying, Sam, to know that I haven't been wasting my time in talking to you. (*Strutting around proudly*)   Tolstoy may have educated his peasants, but I've educated you.

SAM   Standard Four to Standard Nine.

HALLY   Have we been at it as long as that?

SAM   Yep. And my first lesson was geography.

HALLY   (*Intrigued*)   Really? I don't remember.

SAM   My room there at the back of the old Jubilee Boarding House. I had just started working for your Mom. Little boy in short trousers walks in one afternoon and asks me seriously: "Sam, do you want to see South Africa?" Hey man! Sure I wanted to see South Africa!

HALLY   Was that me?

SAM   . . . So the next thing I'm looking at a map you
had just done for homework. It was your first one and
you were very proud of yourself.

HALLY   Go on.

SAM   Then came my first lesson. "Repeat after me, Sam:
Gold in the Transvaal, mealies in the Free State, sugar
in Natal and grapes in the Cape." I still know it!

HALLY   Well, I'll be buggered. So that's how it all
started.

SAM   And your next map was one with all the rivers and
the mountains they came from. The Orange, the Vaal,
the Limpopo, the Zambezi . . .

HALLY   You've got a phenomenal memory!

SAM   You should be grateful. That is why you started
passing your exams. You tried to be better than me.
    (*They laugh together.* WILLIE *is attracted by the
    laughter and joins them*)

HALLY   The old Jubilee Boarding House. Sixteen rooms
with board and lodging, rent in advance and one week's
notice. I haven't thought about it for donkey's years
. . . and I don't think that's an accident. God, was I
glad when we sold it and moved out. Those years are
not remembered as the happiest ones of an unhappy
childhood.

WILLIE   (*Knocking on the table and trying to imitate a
woman's voice*)   "Hally, are you there?"

HALLY   Who's that supposed to be?

WILLIE   "What you doing in there, Hally? Come out at
once!"

HALLY   (*To* SAM)   What's he talking about?

SAM   Don't you remember?

WILLIE "Sam, Willie . . . is he in there with you boys?"

SAM Hiding away in our room when your mother was looking for you.

HALLY (*Another good laugh*) Of course! I used to crawl and hide under your bed! But finish the story, Willie. Then what used to happen? You chaps would give the game away by telling her I was in there with you. So much for friendship.

SAM We couldn't lie to her. She knew.

HALLY Which meant I got another rowing for hanging around the "servants' quarters." I think I spent more time in there with you chaps than anywhere else in that dump. And do you blame me? Nothing but bloody misery wherever you went. Somebody was always complaining about the food, or my mother was having a fight with Micky Nash because she'd caught her with a petty officer in her room. Maud Meiring was another one. Remember those two? They were prostitutes, you know. Soldiers and sailors from the troopships. Bottom fell out of the business when the war ended. God, the flotsam and jetsam that life washed up on our shores! No joking, if it wasn't for your room, I would have been the first certified ten-year-old in medical history. Ja, the memories are coming back now. Walking home from school and thinking: "What can I do this afternoon?" Try out a few ideas, but sooner or later I'd end up in there with you fellows. I bet you I could still find my way to your room with my eyes closed. (*He does exactly that*) Down the corridor . . . telephone on the right, which my Mom keeps locked because somebody is using it on the sly and not paying . . . past the kitchen and unappetizing cooking smells . . . around the corner into the backyard, hold my breath again because there are more smells coming when I pass your lavatory, then into that little passageway, first door on the right and into your room. How's that?

SAM   Good. But, as usual, you forgot to knock.

HALLY   Like that time I barged in and caught you and
   Cynthia . . . at it. Remember? God, was I embar-
   rassed! I didn't know what was going on at first.

SAM   Ja, that taught you a lesson.

HALLY   And about a lot more than knocking on doors,
   I'll have you know, and I don't mean geography either.
   Hell, Sam, couldn't you have waited until it was dark?

SAM   No.

HALLY   Was it that urgent?

SAM   Yes, and if you don't believe me, wait until your
   time comes.

HALLY   No, thank you. I am not interested in girls.
   (*Back to his memories . . . Using a few chairs he recreates the room as he lists the items*)   A gray little
   room with a cold cement floor. Your bed against that
   wall . . . and I now know why the mattress sags so
   much! . . . Willie's bed . . . it's propped up on
   bricks because one leg is broken . . . that wobbly little
   table with the washbasin and jug of water . . . Yes!
   . . . stuck to the wall above it are some pin-up pictures from magazines. Joe Louis . . .

WILLIE   Brown Bomber. World Title.   (*Boxing pose*)
   Three rounds and knockout.

HALLY   Against who?

SAM   Max Schmeling.

HALLY   Correct. I can also remember Fred Astaire and
   Ginger Rogers, and Rita Hayworth in a bathing costume which always made me hot and bothered when I
   looked at it. Under Willie's bed is an old suitcase with
   all his clothes in a mess, which is why I never hide there.
   Your things are neat and tidy in a trunk next to your
   bed, and on it there is a picture of you and Cynthia in

your ballroom clothes, your first silver cup for third place in a competition and an old radio which doesn't work anymore. Have I left out anything?

SAM No.

HALLY Right, so much for the stage directions. Now the characters. (SAM *and* WILLIE *move to their appropriate positions in the bedroom*) Willie is in bed, under his blankets with his clothes on, complaining nonstop about something, but we can't make out a word of what he's saying because he's got his head under the blankets as well. You're on your bed trimming your toenails with a knife—not a very edifying sight—and as for me . . . What am I doing?

SAM You're sitting on the floor giving Willie a lecture about being a good loser while you get the checker board and pieces ready for a game. Then you go to Willie's bed, pull off the blankets and make him play with you first because you know you're going to win, and that gives you the second game with me.

HALLY And you certainly were a bad loser, Willie!

WILLIE Haai!

HALLY Wasn't he, Sam? And so slow! A game with you almost took the whole afternoon. Thank God I gave up trying to teach you how to play chess.

WILLIE You and Sam cheated.

HALLY I never saw Sam cheat, and mine were mostly the mistakes of youth.

WILLIE Then how is it you two was always winning?

HALLY Have you ever considered the possibility, Willie, that it was because we were better than you?

WILLIE Every time better?

HALLY Not every time. There were occasions when we deliberately let you win a game so that you would stop

sulking and go on playing with us. Sam used to wink at me when you weren't looking to show me it was time to let you win.

WILLIE   So then you two didn't play fair.

HALLY   It was for your benefit, Mr. Malopo, which is more than being fair. It was an act of self-sacrifice. (*To* SAM)   But you know what my best memory is, don't you?

SAM   No.

HALLY   Come on, guess. If your memory is so good, you must remember it as well.

SAM   We got up to a lot of tricks in there, Hally.

HALLY   This one was special, Sam.

SAM   I'm listening.

HALLY   It started off looking like another of those useless nothing-to-do afternoons. I'd already been down to Main Street looking for adventure, but nothing had happened. I didn't feel like climbing trees in the Donkin Park or pretending I was a private eye and following a stranger . . . so as usual: See what's cooking in Sam's room. This time it was you on the floor. You had two thin pieces of wood and you were smoothing them down with a knife. It didn't look particularly interesting, but when I asked you what you were doing, you just said, "Wait and see, Hally. Wait . . . and see" . . . in that secret sort of way of yours, so I knew there was a surprise coming. You teased me, you bugger, by being deliberately slow and not answering my questions!
    (SAM *laughs*)
And whistling while you worked away! God, it was infuriating! I could have brained you! It was only when you tied them together in a cross and put that down on the brown paper that I realized what you were doing. "Sam is making a kite?" And when I asked you

and you said "Yes" . . . ! (*Shaking his head with disbelief*) The sheer audacity of it took my breath away. I mean, seriously, what the hell does a black man know about flying a kite? I'll be honest with you, Sam, I had no hopes for it. If you think I was excited and happy, you got another guess coming. In fact, I was shit-scared that we were going to make fools of ourselves. When we left the boarding house to go up onto the hill, I was praying quietly that there wouldn't be any other kids around to laugh at us.

SAM   (*Enjoying the memory as much as* HALLY)   Ja, I could see that.

HALLY   I made it obvious, did I?

SAM   Ja. You refused to carry it.

HALLY   Do you blame me? Can you remember what the poor thing looked like? Tomato-box wood and brown paper! Flour and water for glue! Two of my mother's old stockings for a tail, and then all those bits and pieces of string you made me tie together so that we could fly it! Hell, no, that was now only asking for a miracle to happen.

SAM   Then the big argument when I told you to hold the string and run with it when I let go.

HALLY   I was prepared to run, all right, but straight back to the boarding house.

SAM   (*Knowing what's coming*)   So what happened?

HALLY   Come on, Sam, you remember as well as I do.

SAM   I want to hear it from you.
           (HALLY *pauses. He wants to be as accurate as possible*)

HALLY   You went a little distance from me down the hill, you held it up ready to let it go. . . . "This is it," I thought. "Like everything else in my life, here comes another fiasco." Then you shouted, "Go, Hally!" and

I started to run. (*Another pause*) I don't know how to describe it, Sam. Ja! The miracle happened! I was running, waiting for it to crash to the ground, but instead suddenly there was something alive behind me at the end of the string, tugging at it as if it wanted to be free. I looked back . . . (*Shakes his head*) . . . I still can't believe my eyes. It was flying! Looping around and trying to climb even higher into the sky. You shouted to me to let it have more string. I did, until there was none left and I was just holding that piece of wood we had tied it to. You came up and joined me. You were laughing.

SAM   So were you. And shouting, "It works, Sam! We've done it!"

HALLY   And we had! I was so proud of us! It was the most splendid thing I had ever seen. I wished there were hundreds of kids around to watch us. The part that scared me, though, was when you showed me how to make it dive down to the ground and then just when it was on the point of crashing, swoop up again!

SAM   You didn't want to try yourself.

HALLY   Of course not! I would have been suicidal if anything had happened to it. Watching you do it made me nervous enough. I was quite happy just to see it up there with its tail fluttering behind it. You left me after that, didn't you? You explained how to get it down, we tied it to the bench so that I could sit and watch it, and you went away. I wanted you to stay, you know. I was a little scared of having to look after it by myself.

SAM   (*Quietly*)   I had work to do, Hally.

HALLY   It was sort of sad bringing it down, Sam. And it looked sad again when it was lying there on the ground. Like something that had lost its soul. Just tomato-box wood, brown paper and two of my mother's old stockings! But, hell, I'll never forget that first mo-

ment when I saw it up there. I had a stiff neck the next
day from looking up so much.

(SAM *laughs*. HALLY *turns to him with a question he
never thought of asking before*)

Why did you make that kite, Sam?

SAM (*Evenly*) I can't remember.

HALLY Truly?

SAM Too long ago, Hally.

HALLY Ja, I suppose it was. It's time for another one,
you know.

SAM Why do you say that?

HALLY Because it feels like that. Wouldn't be a good
day to fly it, though.

SAM No. You can't fly kites on rainy days.

HALLY (*He studies* SAM. *Their memories have made him
conscious of the man's presence in his life*) How old
are you, Sam?

SAM Two score and five.

HALLY Strange, isn't it?

SAM What?

HALLY Me and you.

SAM What's strange about it?

HALLY Little white boy in short trousers and a black man
old enough to be his father flying a kite. It's not every
day you see that.

SAM But why strange? Because the one is white and the
other black?

HALLY I don't know. Would have been just as strange, I
suppose, if it had been me and my Dad . . . cripple
man and a little boy! Nope! There's no chance of me
flying a kite without it being strange. (*Simple state-*

ment of fact—no self-pity)   There's a nice little short
story there. "The Kite-Flyers." But we'd have to find a
twist in the ending.

SAM   Twist?

HALLY   Yes. Something unexpected. The way it ended
with us was too straightforward . . . me on the bench
and you going back to work. There's no drama in that.

WILLIE   And me?

HALLY   You?

WILLIE   Yes me.

HALLY   You want to get into the story as well, do you? I
got it! Change the title: "Afternoons in Sam's Room"
. . . expand it and tell all the stories. It's on its way to
being a novel. Our days in the old Jubilee. Sad in a way
that they're over. I almost wish we were still in that little
room.

SAM   We're still together.

HALLY   That's true. It's just that life felt the right size
in there . . . not too big and not too small. Wasn't so
hard to work up a bit of courage. It's got so bloody
complicated since then.
   (*The telephone rings.* SAM *answers it*)

SAM   St. George's Park Tea Room . . . Hello, Madam
. . . Yes, Madam, he's here. . . . Hally, it's your
mother.

HALLY   Where is she phoning from?

SAM   Sounds like the hospital. It's a public telephone.

HALLY   (*Relieved*)   You see! I told you.   (*The telephone*)   Hello, Mom . . . Yes . . . Yes no fine. Everything's under control here. How's things with poor old
Dad? . . . Has he had a bad turn? . . . What? . . .
Oh, God! . . . Yes, Sam told me, but I was sure he'd

made a mistake. But what's this all about, Mom? He didn't look at all good last night. How can he get better so quickly? . . . Then very obviously you must say no. Be firm with him. You're the boss. . . . You know what it's going to be like if he comes home. . . . Well then, don't blame me when I fail my exams at the end of the year. . . . Yes! How am I expected to be fresh for school when I spend half the night massaging his gammy leg? . . . So am I! . . . So tell him a white lie. Say Dr. Colley wants more X-rays of his stump. Or bribe him. We'll sneak in double tots of brandy in future. . . . What? . . . Order him to get back into bed at once! If he's going to behave like a child, treat him like one. . . . All right, Mom! I was just trying to . . . I'm sorry. . . . I said I'm sorry. . . . Quick, give me your number. I'll phone you back. (*He hangs up and waits a few seconds*) Here we go again! (*He dials*) I'm sorry, Mom. . . . Okay . . . But now listen to me carefully. All it needs is for you to put your foot down. Don't take no for an answer. . . . Did you hear me? And whatever you do, don't discuss it with him. . . . Because I'm frightened you'll give in to him. . . . Yes, Sam gave me lunch. . . . I ate all of it! . . . No, Mom not a soul. It's still raining here. . . . Right, I'll tell them. I'll just do some homework and then lock up. . . . But remember now, Mom. Don't listen to anything he says. And phone me back and let me know what happens. . . . Okay. Bye, Mom. (*He hangs up. The men are staring at him*) My Mom says that when you're finished with the floors you must do the windows. (*Pause*) Don't misunderstand me, chaps. All I want is for him to get better. And if he was, I'd be the first person to say: "Bring him home." But he's not, and we can't give him the medical care and attention he needs at home. That's what hospitals are there for. (*Brusquely*) So don't just stand there! Get on with it!

(SAM *clears* HALLY's *table*)

You heard right. My Dad wants to go home.

SAM   Is he better?

HALLY   (*Sharply*)   No! How the hell can he be better when last night he was groaning with pain? This is not an age of miracles!

SAM   Then he should stay in hospital.

HALLY   (*Seething with irritation and frustration*)   Tell me something I don't know, Sam. What the hell do you think I was saying to my Mom? All I can say is fuck-it-all.

SAM   I'm sure he'll listen to your Mom.

HALLY   You don't know what she's up against. He's already packed his shaving kit and pajamas and is sitting on his bed with his crutches, dressed and ready to go. I know him when he gets in that mood. If she tries to reason with him, we've had it. She's no match for him when it comes to a battle of words. He'll tie her up in knots.   (*Trying to hide his true feelings*)

SAM   I suppose it gets lonely for him in there.

HALLY   With all the patients and nurses around? Regular visits from the Salvation Army? Balls! It's ten times worse for him at home. I'm at school and my mother is here in the business all day.

SAM   He's at least got you at night.

HALLY   (*Before he can stop himself*)   And we've got him! Please! I don't want to talk about it anymore. (*Unpacks his school case, slamming down books on the table*)   Life is just a plain bloody mess, that's all. And people are fools.

SAM   Come on, Hally.

HALLY   Yes, they are! They bloody well deserve what they get.

SAM   Then don't complain.

HALLY   Don't try to be clever, Sam. It doesn't suit you. Anybody who thinks there's nothing wrong with this world needs to have his head examined. Just when things are going along all right, without fail someone or something will come along and spoil everything. Somebody should write that down as a fundamental law of the Universe. The principle of perpetual disappointment. If there is a God who created this world, he should scrap it and try again.

SAM   All right, Hally, all right. What you got for homework?

HALLY   Bullshit, as usual. (*Opens an exercise book and reads*) "Write five hundred words describing an annual event of cultural or historical significance."

SAM   That should be easy enough for you.

HALLY   And also plain bloody boring. You know what he wants, don't you? One of their useless old ceremonies. The commemoration of the landing of the 1820 Settlers, or if it's going to be culture, Carols by Candlelight every Christmas.

SAM   It's an impressive sight. Make a good description, Hally. All those candles glowing in the dark and the people singing hymns.

HALLY   And it's called religious hysteria. (*Intense irritation*)   Please, Sam! Just leave me alone and let me get on with it. I'm not in the mood for games this afternoon. And remember my Mom's orders . . . you're to help Willie with the windows. Come on now, I don't want any more nonsense in here.

SAM   Okay, Hally, okay.
        (HALLY *settles down to his homework; determined preparations . . . pen, ruler, exercise book, dictionary, another cake . . . all of which will lead to nothing*)
        (SAM *waltzes over to* WILLIE *and starts to replace tables and chairs. He practices a ballroom step while*

doing so. WILLIE *watches. When* SAM *is finished,* WILLIE *tries*) Good! But just a little bit quicker on the turn and only move in to her after she's crossed over. What about this one?

(*Another step. When* SAM *is finished,* WILLIE *again has a go*)

Much better. See what happens when you just relax and enjoy yourself? Remember that in two weeks' time and you'll be all right.

WILLIE   But I haven't got partner, Boet Sam.

SAM   Maybe Hilda will turn up tonight.

WILLIE   No, Boet Sam. (*Reluctantly*) I gave her a good hiding.

SAM   You mean a bad one.

WILLIE   Good bad one.

SAM   Then you mustn't complain either. Now you pay the price for losing your temper.

WILLIE   I also pay two pounds ten shilling entrance fee.

SAM   They'll refund you if you withdraw now.

WILLIE   (*Appalled*) You mean, don't dance?

SAM   Yes.

WILLIE   No! I wait too long and I practice too hard. If I find me new partner, you think I can be ready in two weeks? I ask Madam for my leave now and we practice every day.

SAM   Quickstep non-stop for two weeks. World record, Willie, but you'll be mad at the end.

WILLIE   No jokes, Boet Sam.

SAM   I'm not joking.

WILLIE   So then what?

SAM Find Hilda. Say you're sorry and promise you won't beat her again.

WILLIE No.

SAM Then withdraw. Try again next year.

WILLIE No.

SAM Then I give up.

WILLIE Haaikona, Boet Sam, you can't.

SAM What do you mean, I can't? I'm telling you: I give up.

WILLIE (*Adamant*) No! (*Accusingly*) It was you who start me ballroom dancing.

SAM So?

WILLIE Before that I use to be happy. And is you and Miriam who bring me to Hilda and say here's partner for you.

SAM What are you saying, Willie?

WILLIE You!

SAM But me what? To blame?

WILLIE Yes.

SAM Willie . . . ? (*Bursts into laughter*)

WILLIE And now all you do is make jokes at me. You wait. When Miriam leaves you is my turn to laugh. Ha! Ha! Ha!

SAM (*He can't take* WILLIE *seriously any longer*) She can leave me tonight! I know what to do. (*Bowing before an imaginary partner*) May I have the pleasure? (*He dances and sings*)
"Just a fellow with his pillow . . .
Dancin' like a willow . . .
In an autumn breeze . . ."

WILLIE   There you go again!
    (SAM *goes on dancing and singing*)
Boet Sam!

SAM   There's the answer to your problem! Judges' announcement in two weeks' time: "Ladies and gentlemen, the winner in the open section . . . Mr. Willie Malopo and his pillow!"
    (*This is too much for a now really angry* WILLIE. *He goes for* SAM, *but the latter is too quick for him and puts* HALLY'S *table between the two of them*)

HALLY   (*Exploding*)   For Christ's sake, you two!

WILLIE   (*Still trying to get at* SAM)   I donner you, Sam! Struesgod!

SAM   (*Still laughing*)   Sorry, Willie . . . Sorry . . .

HALLY   Sam! Willie!   (*Grabs his ruler and gives* WILLIE *a vicious whack on the bum*)   How the hell am I supposed to concentrate with the two of you behaving like bloody children!

WILLIE   Hit him too!

HALLY   Shut up, Willie.

WILLIE   He started jokes again.

HALLY   Get back to your work. You too, Sam.   (*His ruler*)   Do you want another one, Willie?
    (SAM *and* WILLIE *return to their work.* HALLY *uses the opportunity to escape from his unsuccessful attempt at homework. He struts around like a little despot, ruler in hand, giving vent to his anger and frustration*)
Suppose a customer had walked in then? Or the Park Superintendent. And seen the two of you behaving like a pair of hooligans. That would have been the end of my mother's license, you know. And your jobs! Well, this is the end of it. From now on there will be no more of your ballroom nonsense in here. This is a business establishment, not a bloody New Brighton dancing

school. I've been far too lenient with the two of you. (*Behind the counter for a green cool drink and a dollop of ice cream. He keeps up his tirade as he prepares it*) But what really makes me bitter is that I allow you chaps a little freedom in here when business is bad and what do you do with it? The foxtrot! Specially you, Sam. There's more to life than trotting around a dance floor and I thought at least you knew it.

SAM It's a harmless pleasure, Hally. It doesn't hurt anybody.

HALLY It's also a rather simple one, you know.

SAM You reckon so? Have you ever tried?

HALLY Of course not.

SAM Why don't you? Now.

HALLY What do you mean? Me dance?

SAM Yes. I'll show you a simple step—the waltz—then you try it.

HALLY What will that prove?

SAM That it might not be as easy as you think.

HALLY I didn't say it was easy. I said it was simple—like in simple-minded, meaning mentally retarded. You can't exactly say it challenges the intellect.

SAM It does other things.

HALLY Such as?

SAM Make people happy.

HALLY (*The glass in his hand*) So do American cream sodas with ice cream. For God's sake, Sam, you're not asking me to take ballroom dancing serious, are you?

SAM Yes.

HALLY (*Sigh of defeat*) Oh, well, so much for trying to give you a decent education. I've obviously achieved nothing.

SAM   You still haven't told me what's wrong with admiring something that's beautiful and then trying to do it yourself.

HALLY   Nothing. But we happen to be talking about a foxtrot, not a thing of beauty.

SAM   But that is just what I'm saying. If you were to see two champions doing, two masters of the art . . . !

HALLY   Oh, God, I give up. So now it's also art!

SAM   Ja.

HALLY   There's a limit, Sam. Don't confuse art and entertainment.

SAM   So then what is art?

HALLY   You want a definition?

SAM   Ja.

HALLY   (*He realizes he has got to be careful. He gives the matter a lot of thought before answering*)   Philosophers have been trying to do that for centuries. What is Art? What is Life? But basically I suppose it's . . . the giving of meaning to matter.

SAM   Nothing to do with beautiful?

HALLY   It goes beyond that. It's the giving of form to the formless.

SAM   Ja, well, maybe it's not art, then. But I still say it's beautiful.

HALLY   I'm sure the word you mean to use is entertaining.

SAM   (*Adamant*)   No. Beautiful. And if you want proof, come along to the Centenary Hall in New Brighton in two weeks' time.
      (*The mention of the Centenary Hall draws* WILLIE *over to them*)

HALLY   What for? I've seen the two of you prancing around in here often enough.

SAM   (*He laughs*)   This isn't the real thing, Hally. We're just playing around in here.

HALLY   So? I can use my imagination.

SAM   And what do you get?

HALLY   A lot of people dancing around and having a so-called good time.

SAM   That all?

HALLY   Well, basically it is that, surely.

SAM   No, it isn't. Your imagination hasn't helped you at all. There's a lot more to it than that. We're getting ready for the championships, Hally, not just another dance. There's going to be a lot of people, all right, and they're going to have a good time, but they'll only be spectators, sitting around and watching. It's just the competitors out there on the dance floor. Party decorations and fancy lights all around the walls! The ladies in beautiful evening dresses!

HALLY   My mother's got one of those, Sam, and, quite frankly, it's an embarrassment every time she wears it.

SAM   (*Undeterred*)   Your imagination left out the excitement.
    (HALLY *scoffs*)
Oh, yes. The finalists are not going to be out there just to have a good time. One of those couples will be the 1950 Eastern Province Champions. And your imagination left out the music.

WILLIE   Mr. Elijah Gladman Guzana and his Orchestral Jazzonions.

SAM   The sound of the big band, Hally. Trombone, trumpet, tenor and alto sax. And then, finally, your imagination also left out the climax of the evening when the dancing is finished, the judges have stopped whispering among themselves and the Master of Ceremonies collects their scorecards and goes up onto the stage to announce the winners.

HALLY   All right. So you make it sound like a bit of a
do. It's an occasion. Satisfied?

SAM   (*Victory*)   So you admit that!

HALLY   Emotionally yes, intellectually no.

SAM   Well, I don't know what you mean by that, all I'm
telling you is that it is going to be *the* event of the
year in New Brighton. It's been sold out for two weeks
already. There's only standing room left. We've got
competitors coming from Kingwilliamstown, East London, Port Alfred.
       (HALLY *starts pacing thoughtfully*)

HALLY   Tell me a bit more.

SAM   I thought you weren't interested . . . intellectually.

HALLY   (*Mysteriously*)   I've got my reasons.

SAM   What do you want to know?

HALLY   It takes place every year?

SAM   Yes. But only every third year in New Brighton.
It's East London's turn to have the championships
next year.

HALLY   Which, I suppose, makes it an even more significant event.

SAM   Ah ha! We're getting somewhere. Our "occasion"
is now a "significant event."

HALLY   I wonder.

SAM   What?

HALLY   I wonder if I would get away with it.

SAM   But what?

HALLY   (*To the table and his exercise book*)   "Write
five hundred words describing an annual event of cultural or historical significance." Would I be stretching

poetic license a little too far if I called your ballroom championships a cultural event?

SAM   You mean . . . ?

HALLY   You think we could get five hundred words out of it, Sam?

SAM   Victor Sylvester has written a whole book on ballroom dancing.

WILLIE   You going to write about it, Master Hally?

HALLY   Yes, gentlemen, that is precisely what I am considering doing. Old Doc Bromely—he's my English teacher—is going to argue with me, of course. He doesn't like natives. But I'll point out to him that in strict anthropological terms the culture of a primitive black society includes its dancing and singing. To put my thesis in a nutshell: The war-dance has been replaced by the waltz. But it still amounts to the same thing: the release of primitive emotions through movement. Shall we give it a go?

SAM   I'm ready.

WILLIE   Me also.

HALLY   Ha! This will teach the old bugger a lesson. (*Decision taken*)   Right. Let's get ourselves organized.   (*This means another cake on the table. He sits*) I think you've given me enough general atmosphere, Sam, but to build the tension and suspense I need facts. (*Pencil poised*)

WILLIE   Give him facts, Boet Sam.

HALLY   What you called the climax . . . how many finalists?

SAM   Six couples.

HALLY   (*Making notes*)   Go on. Give me the picture.

SAM   Spectators seated right around the hall.   (WILLIE *becomes a spectator*)

HALLY . . . and it's a full house.

SAM At one end, on the stage, Gladman and his Orchestral Jazzonions. At the other end is a long table with
the three judges. The six finalists go onto the dance
floor and take up their positions. When they are ready
and the spectators have settled down, the Master of
Ceremonies goes to the microphone. To start with, he
makes some jokes to get the people laughing . . .

HALLY Good touch! (*As he writes*) ". . . creating a
relaxed atmosphere which will change to one of tension
and drama as the climax is approached."

SAM (*Onto a chair to act out the M.C.*) "Ladies and
gentlemen, we come now to the great moment you have
all been waiting for this evening. . . . The finals of
the 1950 Eastern Province Open Ballroom Dancing
Championships. But first let me introduce the finalists!
Mr. and Mrs. Welcome Tchabalala from Kingwilliamstown . . ."

WILLIE (*He applauds after every name*) Is when the
people clap their hands and whistle and make a lot of
noise, Master Hally.

SAM "Mr. Mulligan Njikelane and Miss Nomhle Nkon-
yeni of Grahamstown; Mr. and Mrs. Norman Nchinga
from Port Alfred; Mr. Fats Bokolane and Miss Dina
Plaatjies from East London; Mr. Sipho Dugu and
Mrs. Mable Magada from Peddie; and from New
Brighton our very own Mr. Willie Malopo and Miss
Hilda Samuels."
  (WILLIE *can't believe his ears. He abandons his role
  as spectator and scrambles into position as a finalist*)

WILLIE Relaxed and ready to romance!

SAM The applause dies down. When everybody is silent,
Gladman lifts up his sax, nods at the Orchestral Jazzonions . . .

WILLIE Play the jukebox please, Boet Sam!

SAM   I also only got bus fare, Willie.

HALLY   Hold it, everybody.   (*Heads for the cash register behind the counter*)   How much is in the till, Sam?

SAM   Three shillings. Hally . . . your Mom counted it before she left.
    (HALLY *hesitates*)

HALLY   Sorry, Willie. You know how she carried on the last time I did it. We'll just have to pool our combined imaginations and hope for the best.   (*Returns to the table*)   Back to work. How are the points scored, Sam?

SAM   Maximum of ten points each for individual style, deportment, rhythm and general appearance.

WILLIE   Must I start?

HALLY   Hold it for a second, Willie. And penalties?

SAM   For what?

HALLY   For doing something wrong. Say you stumble or bump into somebody . . . do they take off any points?

SAM   (*Aghast*)   Hally . . . !

HALLY   When you're dancing. If you and your partner collide into another couple.
    (HALLY *can get no further*. SAM *has collapsed with laughter. He explains to* WILLIE)

SAM   If me and Miriam bump into you and Hilda . . .
    (WILLIE *joins him in another good laugh*)
Hally, Hally . . . !

HALLY   (*Perplexed*)   Why? What did I say?

SAM   There's no collisions out there, Hally. Nobody trips or stumbles or bumps into anybody else. That's what that moment is all about. To be one of those finalists on that dance floor is like . . . like being in a dream about a world in which accidents don't happen.

HALLY (*Genuinely moved by* SAM'S *image*) Jesus,
Sam! That's beautiful!

WILLIE (*Can endure waiting no longer*) I'm starting!
(WILLIE *dances while* SAM *talks*)

SAM Of course it is. That's what I've been trying to say
to you all afternoon. And it's beautiful because that
is what we want life to be like. But instead, like you
said, Hally, we're bumping into each other all the
time. Look at the three of us this afternoon: I've bumped
into Willie, the two of us have bumped into you, you've
bumped into your mother, she bumping into your Dad.
. . . None of us knows the steps and there's no music
playing. And it doesn't stop with us. The whole world
is doing it all the time. Open a newspaper and what do
you read? America has bumped into Russia, England
is bumping into India, rich man bumps into poor man.
Those are big collisions, Hally. They make for a lot of
bruises. People get hurt in all that bumping, and we're
sick and tired of it now. It's been going on for too long.
Are we never going to get it right? . . . Learn to dance
life like champions instead of always being just a
bunch of beginners at it?

HALLY (*Deep and sincere admiration of the man*)
You've got a vision, Sam!

SAM Not just me. What I'm saying to you is that everybody's got it. That's why there's only standing room
left for the Centenary Hall in two weeks' time. For as
long as the music lasts, we are going to see six couples
get it right, the way we want life to be.

HALLY But is that the best we can do, Sam . . . watch
six finalists dreaming about the way it should be?

SAM I don't know. But it starts with that. Without the
dream we won't know what we're going for. And anyway I reckon there are a few people who have got past
just dreaming about it and are trying for something

real. Remember that thing we read once in the paper
about the Mahatma Gandhi? Going without food to
stop those riots in India?

HALLY   You're right. He certainly was trying to teach
people to get the steps right.

SAM   And the Pope.

HALLY   Yes, he's another one. Our old General Smuts as
well, you know. He's also out there dancing. You know,
Sam, when you come to think of it, that's what the
United Nations boils down to . . . a dancing school
for politicians!

SAM   And let's hope they learn.

HALLY   (*A little surge of hope*)   You're right. We
mustn't despair. Maybe there's some hope for mankind
after all. Keep it up, Willie.   (*Back to his table with
determination*)   This is a lot bigger than I thought. So
what have we got? Yes, our title: "A World Without
Collisions."

SAM   That sounds good! "A World Without Collisions."

HALLY   Subtitle: "Global Politics on the Dance Floor."
No. A bit too heavy, hey? What about "Ballroom
Dancing as a Political Vision"?
   (*The telephone rings.* SAM *answers it*)

SAM   St. George's Park Tea Room . . . Yes, Madam
. . . Hally, it's your Mom.

HALLY   (*Back to reality*)   Oh, God, yes! I'd forgotten
all about that. Shit! Remember my words, Sam? Just
when you're enjoying yourself, someone or something
will come along and wreck everything.

SAM   You haven't heard what she's got to say yet.

HALLY   Public telephone?

SAM   No.

HALLY   Does she sound happy or unhappy?

SAM   I couldn't tell. (*Pause*)   She's waiting, Hally.

HALLY (*To the telephone*) Hello, Mom . . . No, everything is okay here. Just doing my homework. . . . What's your news? . . . You've what? . . . (*Pause. He takes the receiver away from his ear for a few seconds. In the course of HALLY's telephone conversation, SAM and WILLIE discretely position the stacked tables and chairs. HALLY places the receiver back to his ear*) Yes, I'm still here. Oh, well, I give up now. Why did you do it, Mom? . . . Well, I just hope you know what you've let us in for. . . . (*Loudly*) I said I hope you know what you've let us in for! It's the end of the peace and quiet we've been having. (*Softly*) Where is he? (*Normal voice*) He can't hear us from in there. But for God's sake, Mom, what happened? I told you to be firm with him. . . . Then you and the nurses should have held him down, taken his crutches away. . . . I know only too well he's my father! . . . I'm not being disrespectful, but I'm sick and tired of emptying stinking chamberpots full of phlegm and piss. . . . Yes, I do! When you're not there, he asks *me* to do it. . . . If you really want to know the truth, that's why I've got no appetite for my food. . . . Yes! There's a lot of things you don't know about. For your information, I still haven't got that science textbook I need. And you know why? He borrowed the money you gave me for it. . . . Because I didn't want to start another fight between you two. . . . He says that every time. . . . All right, Mom! (*Viciously*) Then just remember to start hiding your bag away again, because he'll be at your purse before long for money for booze. And when he's well enough to come down here, you better keep an eye on the till as well, because that is also going to develop a leak. . . . Then don't complain to me when he starts his old tricks. . . . Yes, you do. I get it from you on one side and from him on the other, and it makes life

hell for me. I'm not going to be the peacemaker anymore. I'm warning you now: when the two of you start fighting again, I'm leaving home. . . . Mom, if you start crying, I'm going to put down the receiver. . . . Okay . . . (*Lowering his voice to a vicious whisper*) Okay, Mom. I heard you. (*Desperate*) No. . . . Because I don't want to. I'll see him when I get home! Mom! . . . (*Pause. When he speaks again, his tone changes completely. It is not simply pretense. We sense a genuine emotional conflict*) Welcome home, chum! . . . What's that? . . . Don't be silly, Dad. You being home is just about the best news in the world. . . . I bet you are. Bloody depressing there with everybody going on about their ailments, hey! . . . How you feeling? . . . Good . . . Here as well, pal. Coming down cats and dogs. . . . That's right. Just the day for a kip and a toss in your old Uncle Ned. . . . Everything's just hunky-dory on my side, Dad. . . . Well, to start with, there's a nice pile of comics for you on the counter. . . . Yes, old Kemple brought them in. *Batman and Robin, Submariner* . . . just your cup of tea . . . I will. . . . Yes, we'll spin a few yarns tonight. . . . Okay, chum, see you in a little while. . . . No, I promise. I'll come straight home. . . . (*Pause—his mother comes back on the phone*) Mom? Okay. I'll lock up now. . . . What? . . . Oh, the brandy . . . Yes, I'll remember! . . . I'll put it in my suitcase now, for God's sake. I know well enough what will happen if he doesn't get it. . . . (*Places a bottle of brandy on the counter*) I *was* kind to him, Mom. I didn't say anything nasty! . . . All right. Bye. (*End of telephone conversation. A desolate* HALLY *doesn't move. A strained silence*)

SAM   (*Quietly*)   That sounded like a bad bump, Hally.

HALLY   (*Having a hard time controlling his emotions. He speaks carefully*)   Mind your own business, Sam.

SAM   Sorry. I wasn't trying to interfere. Shall we carry

on? Hally? (*He indicates the exercise book. No response from* HALLY)

WILLIE (*Also trying*) Tell him about when they give out the cups, Boet Sam.

SAM Ja! That's another big moment. The presentation of the cups after the winners have been announced. You've got to put that in.
(*Still no response from* HALLY)

WILLIE A big silver one, Master Hally, called floating trophy for the champions.

SAM We always invite some big-shot personality to hand them over. Guest of honor this year is going to be His Holiness Bishop Jabulani of the All African Free Zionist Church.
(HALLY *gets up abruptly, goes to his table and tears up the page he was writing on*)

HALLY So much for a bloody world without collisions.

SAM Too bad. It was on its way to being a good composition.

HALLY Let's stop bullshitting ourselves, Sam.

SAM Have we been doing that?

HALLY Yes! That's what all our talk about a decent world has been . . . just so much bullshit.

SAM We did say it was still only a dream.

HALLY And a bloody useless one at that. Life's a fuck-up and it's never going to change.

SAM Ja, maybe that's true.

HALLY There's no maybe about it. It's a blunt and brutal fact. All we've done this afternoon is waste our time.

SAM Not if we'd got your homework done.

HALLY   I don't give a shit about my homework, so, for Christ's sake, just shut up about it. (*Slamming books viciously into his school case*) Hurry up now and finish your work. I want to lock up and get out of here. (*Pause*) And then go where? Home-sweet-fucking-home. Jesus, I hate that word.

  (HALLY *goes to the counter to put the brandy bottle and comics in his school case. After a moment's hesitation, he smashes the bottle of brandy. He abandons all further attempts to hide his feelings.* SAM *and* WILLIE *work away as unobtrusively as possible*)

Do you want to know what is really wrong with your lovely little dream, Sam? It's not just that we are all bad dancers. That does happen to be perfectly true, but there's more to it than just that. You left out the cripples.

SAM   Hally!

HALLY   (*Now totally reckless*) Ja! Can't leave them out, Sam. That's why we always end up on our backsides on the dance floor. They're also out there dancing . . . like a bunch of broken spiders trying to do the quick-step! (*An ugly attempt at laughter*) When you come to think of it, it's a bloody comical sight. I mean, it's bad enough on two legs . . . but one and a pair of crutches! Hell, no, Sam. That's guaranteed to turn that dance floor into a shambles. Why you shaking your head? Picture it, man. For once this afternoon let's use our imaginations sensibly.

SAM   Be careful, Hally.

HALLY   Of what? The truth? I seem to be the only one around here who is prepared to face it. We've had the pretty dream, it's time now to wake up and have a good long look at the way things really are. Nobody knows the steps, there's no music, the cripples are also out there tripping up everybody and trying to get into the act, and it's all called the All-Comers-How-

to-Make-a-Fuckup-of-Life Championships. (*Another ugly laugh*) Hang on, Sam! The best bit is still coming. Do you know what the winner's trophy is? A beautiful big chamber-pot with roses on the side, and it's full to the brim with piss. And guess who I think is going to be this year's winner.

SAM   (*Almost shouting*)   Stop now!

HALLY   (*Suddenly appalled by how far he has gone*) Why?

SAM   Hally? It's your father you're talking about.

HALLY   So?

SAM   Do you know what you've been saying?
        (HALLY *can't answer.* He is rigid with shame. SAM *speaks to him sternly*)
No, Hally, you mustn't do it. Take back those words and ask for forgiveness! It's a terrible sin for a son to mock his father with jokes like that. You'll be punished if you carry on. Your father is your father, even if he is a . . . cripple man.

WILLIE   Yes, Master Hally. Is true what Sam say.

SAM   I understand how you are feeling, Hally, but even so . . .

HALLY   No, you don't!

SAM   I think I do.

HALLY   And I'm telling you you don't. Nobody does. (*Speaking carefully as his shame turns to rage at* SAM) It's your turn to be careful, Sam. Very careful! You're treading on dangerous ground. Leave me and my father alone.

SAM   I'm not the one who's been saying things about him.

HALLY   What goes on between me and my Dad is none of your business!

SAM   Then don't tell me about it. If that's all you've got to say about him, I don't want to hear.
(*For a moment* HALLY *is at loss for a response*)

HALLY   Just get on with your bloody work and shut up.

SAM   Swearing at me won't help you.

HALLY   Yes, it does! Mind your own fucking business and shut up!

SAM   Okay. If that's the way you want it, I'll stop trying.
(*He turns away. This infuriates* HALLY *even more*)

HALLY   Good. Because what you've been trying to do is meddle in something you know nothing about. All that concerns you in here, Sam, is to try and do what you get paid for—keep the place clean and serve the customers. In plain words, just get on with your job. My mother is right. She's always warning me about allowing you to get too familiar. Well, this time you've gone too far. It's going to stop right now.
(*No response from* SAM)
You're only a servant in here, and don't forget it.
(*Still no response.* HALLY *is trying hard to get one*)
And as far as my father is concerned, all you need to remember is that he is your boss.

SAM   (*Needled at last*)   No, he isn't. I get paid by your mother.

HALLY   Don't argue with me, Sam!

SAM   Then don't say he's my boss.

HALLY   He's a white man and that's good enough for you.

SAM   I'll try to forget you said that.

HALLY   Don't! Because you won't be doing me a favor if you do. I'm telling you to remember it.
(*A pause.* SAM *pulls himself together and makes one last effort*)

SAM   Hally, Hally . . . ! Come on now. Let's stop be-

fore it's too late. You're right. We *are* on dangerous ground. If we're not careful, somebody is going to get hurt.

HALLY   It won't be me.

SAM   Don't be so sure.

HALLY   I don't know what you're talking about, Sam.

SAM   Yes, you do.

HALLY   (*Furious*)   Jesus, I wish you would stop trying to tell me what I do and what I don't know.
(SAM *gives up. He turns to* WILLIE)

SAM   Let's finish up.

HALLY   Don't turn your back on me! I haven't finished talking.
(*He grabs* SAM *by the arm and tries to make him turn around.* SAM *reacts with a flash of anger*)

SAM   Don't do that, Hally! (*Facing the boy*)   All right, I'm listening. Well? What do you want to say to me?

HALLY   (*Pause as* HALLY *looks for something to say*)   To begin with, why don't you also start calling me Master Harold, like Willie.

SAM   Do you mean that?

HALLY   Why the hell do you think I said it?

SAM   And if I don't?

HALLY   You might just lose your job.

SAM   (*Quietly and very carefully*)   If you make me say it once, I'll never call you anything else again.

HALLY   So?   (*The boy confronts the man*)   Is that meant to be a threat?

SAM   Just telling you what will happen if you make me do that. You must decide what it means to you.

HALLY   Well, I have. It's good news. Because that is exactly what Master Harold wants from now on. Think of
it as a little lesson in respect, Sam, that's long overdue,
and I hope you remember it as well as you do your
geography. I can tell you now that somebody who will
be glad to hear I've finally given it to you will be my
Dad. Yes! He agrees with my Mom. He's always going
on about it as well. "You must teach the boys to show
you more respect, my son."

SAM   So now you can stop complaining about going home.
Everybody is going to be happy tonight.

HALLY   That's perfectly correct. You see, you mustn't
get the wrong idea about me and my Dad, Sam. We also
have our good times together. Some bloody good laughs.
He's got a marvelous sense of humor. Want to know
what our favorite joke is? He gives out a big groan,
you see, and says: "It's not fair, is it, Hally?" Then I
have to ask: "What, chum?" And then he says: "A
nigger's arse" . . . and we both have a good laugh.
    (*The men stare at him with disbelief*)
What's the matter, Willie? Don't you catch the joke?
You always were a bit slow on the uptake. It's what is
called a pun. You see, fair means both light in color and
to be just and decent.   (*He turns to* SAM)   I thought
you would catch it, Sam.

SAM   Oh ja, I catch it all right.

HALLY   But it doesn't appeal to your sense of humor.

SAM   Do you really laugh?

HALLY   Of course.

SAM   To please him? Make him feel good?

HALLY   No, for heaven's sake! I laugh because I think it's
a bloody good joke.

SAM   You're really trying hard to be ugly, aren't you?
And why drag poor old Willie into it? He's done nothing to you except show you the respect you want so

badly. That's also not being fair, you know . . . and *I* mean just or decent.

WILLIE   It's all right, Sam. Leave it now.

SAM   It's me you're after. You should just have said "Sam's arse" . . . because that's the one you're trying to kick. Anyway, how do you know it's not fair? You've never seen it. Do you want to?   (*He drops his trousers and underpants and presents his backside for* HALLY'*s inspection*)   Have a good look. A real Basuto arse . . . which is about as nigger as they can come. Satisfied?   (*Trousers up*)   Now you can make your Dad even happier when you go home tonight. Tell him I showed you my arse and he is quite right. It's not fair. And if it will give him an even better laugh next time, I'll also let *him* have a look. Come, Willie, let's finish up and go.

   (SAM *and* WILLIE *start to tidy up the tea room.* HALLY *doesn't move. He waits for a moment when* SAM *passes him*)

HALLY   (*Quietly*)   Sam . . .
   (SAM *stops and looks expectantly at the boy.* HALLY *spits in his face. A long and heartfelt groan from* WILLIE. *For a few seconds* SAM *doesn't move*)

SAM   (*Taking out a handkerchief and wiping his face*) It's all right, Willie.
   (*To* HALLY)
Ja, well, you've done it . . . Master Harold. Yes, I'll start calling you that from now on. It won't be difficult anymore. You've hurt yourself, Master Harold. I saw it coming. I warned you, but you wouldn't listen. You've just hurt yourself *bad*. And you're a coward, Master Harold. The face you should be spitting in is your father's . . . but you used mine, because you think you're safe inside your fair skin . . . and this time I don't mean just or decent.   (*Pause, then moving violently towards* HALLY)   Should I hit him, Willie?

WILLIE   (*Stopping* SAM)   No, Boet Sam.

SAM   (*Violently*)   Why not?

WILLIE   It won't help, Boet Sam.

SAM   I don't want to help! I want to hurt him.

WILLIE   You also hurt yourself.

SAM   And if he had done it to you, Willie?

WILLIE   Me? Spit at me like I was a dog?   (*A thought that had not occurred to him before. He looks at* HALLY) Ja. Then I want to hit him. I want to hit him hard!
    (*A dangerous few seconds as the men stand staring at the boy.* WILLIE *turns away, shaking his head*) But maybe all I do is go cry at the back. He's little boy, Boet Sam. Little *white* boy. Long trousers now, but he's still little boy.

SAM   (*His violence ebbing away into defeat as quickly as it flooded*)   You're right. So go on, then: groan again, Willie. You do it better than me.   (*To* HALLY)   You don't know all of what you've just done . . . Master Harold. It's not just that you've made me feel dirtier than I've ever been in my life . . . I mean, how do I wash off yours and your father's filth? . . . I've also failed. A long time ago I promised myself I was going to try and do something, but you've just shown me . . . Master Harold . . . that I've failed.   (*Pause*) I've also got a memory of a little white boy when he was still wearing short trousers and a black man, but they're not flying a kite. It was the old Jubilee days, after dinner one night. I was in my room. You came in and just stood against the wall, looking down at the ground, and only after I'd asked you what you wanted, what was wrong, I don't know how many times, did you speak and even then so softly I almost didn't hear you. "Sam, please help me to go and fetch my Dad." Remember? He was dead drunk on the floor of the Central Hotel Bar. They'd phoned for your Mom, but you were the only one at home. And do you remember how we did it? You went in first by yourself to ask permission for me

to go into the bar. Then I loaded him onto my back like a baby and carried him back to the boarding house with you following behind carrying his crutches. (*Shaking his head as he remembers*) A crowded Main Street with all the people watching a little white boy following his drunk father on a nigger's back! I felt for that little boy . . . Master Harold. I felt for him. After that we still had to clean him up, remember? He'd messed in his trousers, so we had to clean him up and get him into bed.

HALLY (*Great pain*) I love him, Sam.

SAM I know you do. That's why I tried to stop you from saying these things about him. It would have been so simple if you could have just despised him for being a weak man. But he's your father. You love him and you're ashamed of him. You're ashamed of so much! . . . And now that's going to include yourself. That was the promise I made to myself: to try and stop that happening. (*Pause*) After we got him to bed you came back with me to my room and sat in a corner and carried on just looking down at the ground. And for days after that! You hadn't done anything wrong, but you went around as if you owed the world an apology for being alive. I didn't like seeing that! That's not the way a boy grows up to be a man! . . . But the one person who should have been teaching you what that means was the cause of your shame. If you really want to know, that's why I made you that kite. I wanted you to look up, be proud of something, of yourself . . . (*Bitter smile at the memory*) . . . and you certainly were that when I left you with it up there on the hill. Oh, ja . . . something else! . . . If you ever do write it as a short story, there *was* a twist in our ending. I couldn't sit down there and stay with you. It was a "Whites Only" bench. You were too young, too excited to notice then. But not anymore. If you're not careful . . . Master Harold . . . you're going to be sitting up there by yourself for a long time to come, and there won't be

a kite in the sky.   (SAM *has got nothing more to say.
He exits into the kitchen, taking off his waiter's jacket*)

WILLIE   Is bad. Is all all bad in here now.

HALLY   (*Books into his school case, raincoat on*)   Willie
. . .   (*It is difficult to speak*)   Will you lock up for
me and look after the keys?

WILLIE   Okay.
(SAM *returns.* HALLY *goes behind the counter and
collects the few coins in the cash register. As he starts
to leave . . .*)

SAM   Don't forget the comic books.
(HALLY *returns to the counter and puts them in his
case. He starts to leave again*)

SAM   (*To the retreating back of the boy*)   Stop . . .
Hally . . .
(HALLY *stops, but doesn't turn to face him*)
Hally . . . I've got no right to tell you what being a
man means if I don't behave like one myself, and I'm
not doing so well at that this afternoon. Should we try
again, Hally?

HALLY   Try what?

SAM   Fly another kite, I suppose. It worked once, and
this time I need it as much as you do.

HALLY   It's still raining, Sam. You can't fly kites on
rainy days, remember.

SAM   So what do we do? Hope for better weather to-
morrow?

HALLY   (*Helpless gesture*)   I don't know. I don't know
anything anymore.

SAM   You sure of that, Hally? Because it would be pretty
hopeless if that was true. It would mean nothing has
been learnt in here this afternoon, and there was a hell
of a lot of teaching going on . . . one way or the other.
But anyway, I don't believe you. I reckon there's one

thing you know. You don't *have* to sit up there by your-self. You know what that bench means now, and you can leave it any time you choose. All you've got to do is stand up and walk away from it.

(HALLY *leaves.* WILLIE *goes up quietly to* SAM)

WILLIE   Is okay, Boet Sam. You see. Is . . .   (*He can't find any better words*)   . . . *is* going to be okay to-morrow. (*Changing his tone*) Hey, Boet Sam! (*He is trying hard*)   You right. I think about it and you right. Tonight I find Hilda and say sorry. And make promise I won't beat her no more. You hear me, Boet Sam?

SAM   I hear you, Willie.

WILLIE   And when we practice I relax and romance with her from beginning to end. Non-stop! You watch! Two weeks' time: "First prize for promising newcomers: Mr. Willie Malopo and Miss Hilda Samuels." (*Sudden impulse*)   To hell with it! I walk home.   (*He goes to the jukebox, puts in a coin and selects a record. The machine comes to life in the gray twilight, blushing its way through a spectrum of soft, romantic colors*)   How did you say it, Boet Sam? Let's dream.   (WILLIE *sways with the music and gestures for* SAM *to dance*)

(*Sarah Vaughan sings*)
"Little man you're crying,
I know why you're blue,
Someone took your kiddy car away;
Better go to sleep now,
Little man you've had a busy day."   (*etc. etc.*)
    You lead. I follow.
    (*The men dance together*)
"Johnny won your marbles,
Tell you what we'll do;
Dad will get you new ones
    right away;
Better go to sleep now,
Little man you've had a
    busy day."